The Farewell Discourses in Practice

Practice Interpretation

4

ISSN 2048-0431

Deo Publishing

The FAREWELL DISCOURSES *in* PRACTICE

Edited by

John Vincent

deo
PUBLISHING

BLANDFORD FORUM

Practice Interpretation series, 4

ISSN 2048-0431

Copyright © 2015 Deo Publishing
P.O. Box 6284, Blandford Forum, Dorset DT11 1AQ, UK

Printed by Henry Ling Ltd, at the Dorset Press, Dorchester, DT1 1HD, UK

British Library Cataloguing-in-Publication data
A catalogue record for this book is available from the British Library

ISBN 978-1-905679-33-1

Contents

Preface 7
The Contributors 8

Chapter 1
Practice Interpretation: An Update
John Vincent 11

Chapter 2
John's Gospel and Practice Interpretation
John Vincent 15

Chapter 3
Footwashing and Diaconal Ordination
Leslie Francis 21

Chapter 4
Sin, Righteousness and Judgment
David Blatherwick 29

Chapter 5
Friendship in John 15 in the Legal Workplace
Sarah Pullin 37

Chapter 6
Judas, the Common Purse and the Poor
David McLoughlin 49

Chapter 7
Farewell Discourses as Retrospective Testimony
Ian Wallis 55

Chapter 8
The Practice of Divinity in Disciples
John Vincent 65

Chapter 9
Jesus' Recall to Discipleship in John 21
Nirmal Fernando 73

Chapter 10
Charter of Cultural Liberation
Alan Saxby..83

A Practice Interpretation Bibliography 91

Index of Subjects and Names...93

Preface

John Rogerson's edited *Leviticus in Practice* is now followed by a determined and at times idiosyncratic set of attempts at the central chapters of John's Gospel. The encounter proved to be unexpectedly and provocatively productive, as readers now see.

Our next volume, with Old and New Testament pieces, will be on *The Servant of God*. Beyond that, our July meeting of 2015 sees us working at the scriptural and contemporary elements of *Discipleship* – a newly urged focus for Anglicans in a February 2015 Report.

Most of our work is done at the July Summer School of the Urban Theology Unit. Having moved in 2014 from our former home in Abbeyfield Road, we now meet at our new base in the centre of Sheffield.

Readers interested in joining us would be most welcome. Please contact us at the address below:

John J. Vincent
Urban Theology Unit
Victoria Hall
Norfolk Street
Sheffield S1 2JB

John J. Vincent
March 2015

Contributors

David Blatherwick is a retired Methodist minister, who served in several mainly urban circuits in England and briefly as Ecumenical Officer for England for the British Council of Churches. His main study interest is Mark's Gospel, but he also has an interest in John's Gospel, mainly because he finds it so difficult to understand. He contributed to the earlier volume, *Stilling the Storm*.

Nirmal Fernando is a lawyer. Sole identity is seen, he says, as discipleship community life – Jesus' and the Buddha's. He has experience in Benedictine monasticism, in Buddhist texts and meditation under Buddhist masters in Sri Lanka and at SOAS. Ashram Community facilitates his organising of the Multifaith Chapel and Library at Burngreave Ashram, Sheffield. A trustee of the Community – he is emphatic on home-based praxis – Rock Street Ashram Community House, Sheffield, he has a home in London and a handful of homes in the UK and Sri Lanka.

Leslie Francis is Professor of Religions and Education and Director of the Warwick Religions and Education Research Unit, University of Warwick, England. He also holds visiting Chairs in York St. John University, England, and Glyndwr University, Wales, together with visiting positions in Boston University, USA, and Pretoria University, South Africa. He serves as Canon Theologian and Canon Treasurer at Bangor Cathedral, Wales.

David McLoughlin is Senior Lecturer in Theology at Newman University. He studied at Oscott College, Birmingham, the Gregorian University Rome, Cambridge and UTU Sheffield. A former President of the Catholic Theological Association of Great Britian and Vice President of the European Association of Catholic Theology, his current research is on the changing use of the Scriptures in radical Christian movements. He is a founder member of the Movement of Christian Workers and is currently responsible for its theological resourcing nationally and internationally.

Sarah Pullin has worked as a lawyer for over 20 years, currently in a large multinational firm. Sarah has also recently become an ordained

Anglican priest with the focus of her ministry in the business and work-place. Sarah undertook her ordination training and theological MA in Ministry and Mission at STETS under the supervision of Principal David Holgate. Sarah is married to Stephen and has three sons.

Alan Saxby is a retired Methodist minister. Following Circuit ministry in Leicestershire and South Yorkshire he transferred to a Sector Ministry in Further Education, working as College Counsellor at Barnsley College. Following years of caring for his wife with chronic ME he embarked in his late 60's on a research programme at the University of Sheffield on 'James and the Origin of the Jerusalem Church' (publication pending) for which he was awarded a doctorate in 2014. He was a contributor to the earlier *Stilling the Storm* volume.

John Vincent is Director Emeritus of the Urban Theology Unit, Leader of the Ashram Community, and a doctoral supervisor for the University of Birmingham. Besides editing Practice Interpretation volumes, his most recent publication is *Christ in the City: The Dynamics of Christ in Urban Theological Practice* (Sheffield: Urban Theology Unit, 2013). He has also recently edited *Radical Christianity: Roots and Fruits* (Sheffield: St. Mark's CRC Press, forthcoming 2016), and published a third edition of *Radical Jesus* (Sheffield: Ashram Press, 2015).

Ian Wallis, until recently vicar of St Mark's Church, Broomhill, Sheffield, has taught New Testament and early Christian origins at Cambridge and Durham Universities, as well as on various ministry training programmes including the Northern Ordination Course, where he was Principal. He has published widely in this sphere, including two books: *The Faith of Jesus Christ in Early Christian Traditions* (Cambridge: Cambridge University Press, 1995) and *Holy Saturday Faith: Rediscovering the Legacy of Jesus* (London: SPCK, 2000).

1

Practice Interpretation: An Update

JOHN VINCENT

1. Some Basics

We begin with a rehearsal of some of the basics!

Practice criticism argues that people do not hear or tell stories simply because of their own opinions or beliefs about them, or because of their commitment to the community which holds them dear. They primarily value and tell stories because they have some present interest in those stories, which derives from their present lives of discipleship and community living. Practice criticism seeks to add the actual practices of discipleship and community activity to the elements which determined why certain stories were valued, the shape that those stories were given, and the slants which certain words, phrases and references could acquire because of the interests, activities or functions which characterised the disciple's and the community's life.

Practice is the way the scriptural tradition is carried on in history, because practice was the way in which it originated. The text is the essential 'mediator' from the action behind the biblical passage into the action awaiting contemporary disciples acting in faith.

Put simply, if the gospel describes Jesus' "acts" or "projects", then our interest is with consequent "acts" and "projects", which reflect or are based upon the primary acts and projects. The "imitation" of God or Jesus is transformed from the areas of motive, spirituality and inwardness, with which Christians and churches are so much at home today, into areas of intentional practice, contrary embodiment, prophetic entrepreneurship, and alternative community creation. It seems to us that these are in fact the contemporary equivalents of the divine practice(s) revealed in scripture.

Thus, gospel practice criticism seeks to develop insights into the ways in which the originating practice of God, Jesus, disciples or Christian community recorded in scripture provoke, inspire or support corresponding or identified practice in a disciple/reader's community and discipleship, in early church times, historically and today.

John Rogerson puts it thus:

> Practice interpretation is not about deducing metaphysical propositions from biblical narratives, it is about being attentive to the narrated divine encounter with the human in concrete situations and applying the implications of that encounter to the concrete situations of the world(s) of the interpreter.
>
> Practice interpretation, like literary criticism, can be done in various ways. What is common to all forms of practice interpretation is that it begins from the everyday social conditions of people as they are described in the Bible. It is materialistic, not in the sense of being anti-theological, but in its concern to grapple with the realities of life as they appear in the biblical text and as they confront interpreters in daily life.[1]

2. New Moves in Practice Criticism

At the "Use and Influence" Seminar at the British New Testament Conference in Manchester on 5th September 2014, I spoke on "New Moves in Practice Criticism." I made the attempt to open up three issues which are emerging among colleagues engaged in Practice Criticism work.

1. What hermeneutical methods are employed in Practice Criticism? Is there need for a more developed practice-related hermeneutics, such as the familiar form-redaction-reception methods in literary studies? What are the appropriate hermeneutics of suspicion? Can we import methods elaborated in Urban Theology, where a variety of hermeneutical circles/cycles are used?[2]

2. How can the assumptions and presuppositions of Practice Criticism be received within the literary-dominated academy? How in fact are processes of contextual and practice-based record creation to be set alongside normal contextual and experiential learning used in teaching and study? How can practice – and in scriptural times, history and archaeology – be added to "the basic text" for interpretation purposes?

3. Does the whole area of "use and influence" now appear divided? On the one hand are those who have an intention to "use" a Gospel passage for some practical purpose in discipleship, community or politics, seeing it as an "outworking" of a Gospel story or passage? On the other hand, the concept of "influence" is used to observe the intentional

---

[1] J.W. Rogerson, Introduction, in J.W. Rogerson, ed., *Leviticus in Practice*, Blandford Forum: Deo Publishing, 2014, p. 18.

[2] John J. Vincent, *Christ in the City: The Dynamics of Christ in Urban Theological Practice*, Sheffield: Urban Theology Unit, pp. 47-75.

or unintentional appearance of a Gospel story or passage in art, architecture, drama or writing. Can these two ever meet?

The discussion suggested possible answers:

1. The methods of Biblical and Contemporary Situation Analysis, Practice Analysis, Endogenous Analysis and Political Analysis apply both to the biblical passage and to the contemporary practice. Both were felt to be relevant, and a more systematic development of them was encouraged. The methods of Urban Theology and Urban Theologising could be used for this purpose.[3]

2. The non-reception of Practice Interpretation in the academy was experienced as part of the wider problem that many contemporary teachers and students of New Testament studies only have experience of reading and studying ancient and modern texts, and have no experience of people or communities who see themselves as involved in taking the texts as part of personal or community action. It was remarked that the Urban Theology Unit in Sheffield was perhaps unique in providing just such experience simultaneously of biblical study and experimental practice.

3. It was commented that the "use" of a passage is always an intentional thing, in which an individual or a community sees itself as purposely involved with a text. "Influence" was arguably present in wider societal attitudes and media. No ways between were proposed, and the present uneasy cohabitation of "use" and "influence" looks likely to continue – though some in the academy wished to discover practical ways to involve students in the "use" of passages, with appropriate safeguards.

3. Current Work

The *Expository Times* continues to publish my Practice Studies of chapters of Mark's Gospel. The latest is "Multi-Faith Mission in Mark 5", reflecting on the stories of the Gerasene Demoniac, Jairus, and the Woman with the Bleeding, and how these seem to be similar to experiences in the multi-faith context of the Burngreave Ashram in the inner city of Sheffield.

Meantime, Practice Interpretation colleagues Christopher Rowland and Ian Wallis join others from the Urban Theology Unit and Ashram Community in a "relaunch" of the Gospel Radical Christianity tradition in a new 2016 collection of pieces *Radical Christianity, Roots and Fruits*.[4]

---

[3] John J. Vincent, "Outworkings: Multi-Faith Mission in Mark 5", *Expository Times* 125.3, December 2013, pp. 117-122.

[4] John Vincent, ed., *Radical Christianity: Roots and Fruits*, Sheffield: St. Mark's CRC Press, forthcoming 2016.

Our work continues in the annual three-day July meetings at the Urban Theology Unit in Sheffield. Please contact us if interested in participating.

At the July 2015 meeting, we will share work for the *Discipleship* volume, and determine future work and volumes in the series.

The mini-library of Practice Criticism so far reminds me of hearing Karl Barth joking about himself as "the little old man with his wheelbarrow of books". Despite that, we include at the end a guide to our work to date, confining itself to recent publications.

But first, an interesting parallel from the wider world of academic research, on the "impact" of research. From 2008, the new Research Excellence Framework (REF) of the Higher Education Funding Council for England (HEFCE) determines that for 2008-14, twenty per cent of the score will be decided on the basis of "impact". Impact is defined as "demonstrable benefits to the wider economy and society" and must cover extra-academic "users". Case studies are required to lead to "verifiable and quantifiable transformation of popular perception, discourse, vocabulary, or actual practice (including policy-making and commercial impact)".[5]

An article in the *Church Times* by Catherine Pickstock invites readers to provide "information, verification and quantification of their engagement with and "exploration" and "translation" (to use official terms) of recent academic research".[6]

So we are invited to give evidence as to how our perceptions of theological subjects have been changed by reading an academic "output", but also how our vocabulary, or our policy, or our behaviour, or our practices, have changed or modified in any way, as a result.

Biblical studies have been invited to follow suit!

---

[5] *The New Research Framework*, London: Higher Education Funding Council for England, 2011, p. 10.
[6] *Church Times*, 8 April 2011.

2

John's Gospel and Practice Interpretation

JOHN VINCENT

1. The Use of John's Gospel

The question is, what use did the disciple community for which John's Gospel was written actually put it to? If they read it in their meetings, what practice and practices would they perform on the basis of it?

The "real life situation" which John 13–17 suggests is that of a highly committed, select group, repeating together these intense, repetitive and circumlocutory words, poring over them in a constant ongoing communal reflection which constitutes and repeatedly reconstitutes them as a special, single-minded, consciously constituted intentional community concentrating on living by the repeated words of Jesus, and using them to build up and reveal a hidden inner corporate consciousness which manifests itself in intense love and maturity within, repeated listening and repeating words and actions together, and endearing itself in the world as love despite the world's rejection and hostility.

There is clear intention in John's Jesus "to present Jesus speaking both to 'them' and to us, both acting in the past and in the present/future" (Howard-Brook, p. 344).[1] Some things he did not say previously – concerning future expulsion from faith community and being killed (16.5) – were because he was then still present with them.

The only consolation for disciples when grief fills their heart (16.6) is that the paraklete will replace Jesus as their strengthener (16.7) – something "to your advantage". In 16.8-11 "the paraklete will completely replace Jesus in his role of supporting the disciples in their mission to the world" (Howard-Brook, p. 347). No details are given, except that the whole passion narrative which follows is clearly felt to be a Way that

---

[1] Wes Howard-Brook, *Becoming Children of God. John's Gospel and Radical Discipleship*, Maryknoll, NY: Orbis Books, 1994.

is done first by Jesus and then subsequently by disciples in John's community.

2. A Gospel of Practice?

The long tradition of calling John "the Spiritual Gospel" has led to a presupposition that John is more concerned with essence than appearance, with devotion rather than practice. Thus, Sandra M. Schneider comments on the saying of 17.22: "The glory you gave me I have given them, that they also may be completely one."

> In this passage is summed up the whole message of the Gospel. Its point is to bring those who contemplate the Gospel into a union with Jesus which will plunge them into the depths of God's very life, the life Jesus shares with his Father. There is no question that the purpose of the Gospel is the mystical union of the disciples with Jesus in God through the spirit.[2]

The result is a "Reading for Transformation" which results in meditation and contemplation. The only alternative named is "Exegesis for Information".[3]

However, the whole of 17.23 goes on to incorporate the "glory" not in some spiritual reality but in the realm of concrete practice, which is necessary if others are to notice them, if *the world* is to know that "you have sent me and have loved them even as you loved me". John is concerned to reincarnate "the depths of God's very life" through a continuing imitative Jesus practice which itself imitates God's practice.

Recent scholars have opened up new starts in the Practice model. Was Jesus in John configured at least in part in the model of an angel?[4] Or is Jesus in John best described as an "agent" of God and as "son" because "a man's best agent is his son"?[5] Francis Watson comments:

> It may be that there is today a particular need to hear again the gospel in its distinctly Johannine form – according to which Jesus embodies and enacts a definitive divine incursion into the world that occurs 'vertically from above'.[6]

But maybe we might do even better today with a gospel that tells a story "horizontally from alongside". For such is surely John's story – of

---

[2] Sandra M. Schneider, *Written that You May Believe: Encountering Jesus in the Fourth Gospel*, New York: Crossroad, 1999, 15.

[3] Schneider, 17.

[4] See John Ashton, *Studying John: Approaches to the Fourth Gospel*, Oxford: Clarendon Press. 1994– .

[5] Cf. J.A.T. Robinson, *The Priority of John*, London: SCM Press, 1985, 372-373.

[6] Francis Watson, "The Gospel of John and New Testament Theology", in Christopher Rowland and Christopher Tuckett, eds., *The Nature of New Testament Theology*, Oxford: Blackwell, 2006, 246-262 (239).

the Father who practised his deeds and words in secret, of the Son who is made to stand in front of him, to show forth the Father's otherwise hidden deeds and words, of the Spirit who then takes the Son's deeds and words and shows them to the disciples, and of disciples who then take up and continue the Son's deeds and words in Jesus' imitative and Spirit empowered practice. Such a continuation in the horizontal plane of experience and history is surely the liberating and dynamic activity of Father, Son, Spirit and Disciple which John suggests and opens up.

Certainly, this is Trinitiarian procession rather than Trinitarian succession. And such might be a more credible way of enacting a gospel for which today there is a particular need. Few new takers are found for hearing "Das Wort von Oben", the Word from Above. But many seek and find words and actions, lovingly between friends, who pass on the continuing incarnate way of life, love, truth, and healing – in political and communal as well as personal spheres. It is "Das Wort von Unten", the Word from Below, or even better "Das Wort von Seite", the Word from Alongside, which is the Word which we are hearing today.

John helps us and even leads us along these lines.

The Paraclete of John 14.25, whatever the preferred translation, derives from two words – *para*, meaning alongside, parallel to something or someone else, and *kletos*, "called one", from *kaleo*, meaning to call or summon. It is a sideways or alongside operation, a handing-on, that is at the word's root. All the suggested translations like advocate, or comforter, or helper, derive from the position of being alongside. A horizontal ministry!

3. Johannine Practice Interpretation

The key element and dynamic in the Johannine practice reflections in this volume is that John's Gospel sometimes explicitly, often implicitly, sets forth a continuing Jesus-style practice by Jesus' followers, in the gospel time, in the longer term behaviour of early Christian communities, and in contemporary Christian disciples and communities today.

Each contributor indicates this at work in very different contexts and happenings.

Leslie Francis reveals how a person's psychological type preferences influence or determine what one actually does with a text or passage. He describes how a dominant sensing group pick up that the newly ordained deacons "will be doing things that other people do not expect you to be doing, and doing things that you do not expect yourself to be doing", and thus to be "a conduit of God's grace", manifest in the practice of leadership, the costliness of service, and the idea of the servant leader.

David Blatherwick critiques everyday ideas then and now. Sin is sticking to old ways rather than the Kingdom, righteousness is upholding our distinctiveness and loyalty to the law, and judgment is something in the future rather than the present. Rather, our practice must take its key from opposite presuppositions, which John's Jesus acts by and opens up for us.

Sarah Pullin describes the problems of practising friendship on the model of Jesus among lawyers. Friendship gets harder, the more senior you become. But proper care of the self holds this as important, even within a predominantly autonomous and unsociable profession, which is hierarchical to boot, and secretive, competitive, and "up or out". Friendship emerges as a truly counter-cultural activity, not without its dangers to the would-be friend. Could we not parallel much of this among church or academy leaders?

David McLoughlin studies the Johannine records concerning the common purse and donations for the poor, and estimates how far these continue existing Essene community practices. Judas's failure has to be seen in this light. And we have to ask how far the traditions of common purse and treasuries for the poor provide workable models for our finance-preoccupied society and church, pioneered and surpassed in our contemporary Christian practices of Free Meals and Food Banks.

Ian Wallis's reading of John 14 shows how the disciples are prepared to "intuit a 'spiritual persona' or 'alter ego', mediating Jesus' presence by acting as a source of guidance, inspiration, and remembrance, discrete from themselves and capable of maintaining his accessibility". "Jesus was experienced spiritually as a dynamic presence after the crucifixion." But this was a case of "practice engendered presence", rather than "presence engendered practice". So, today "fresh performances of his ministry and imaginative improvisations of his way" bring Jesus to life.

John Vincent sees the crucial contributions of John in his whole theological/Christological narrative, wherein Jesus embodies/replicates God, Spirit embodies/replicates Jesus, and Disciples embody/replicate Spirit. The works of the Father are imitated and done by the Son and are continued by the Spirit in the works of Disciples – a Quaternity rather than a Trinity. The clue to divinity today is thus in the practice of contemporary disciples.

Nirmal Fernando rehearses how John 21 indicates the methods whereby the life and practice of Jesus is re-assembled after the resurrection – socio-economic sharing, sole reliance on Jesus, discipleship community and mutual caring. Nirmal sees similar elements in the Buddha's farewell discourse – discipleship and community, preparedness for separation, continuing community, leadership provisions, and parting words of love. Similar practice interpretations are still active in intentional communities today.

Alan Saxby wants us to stand on the shoulders of John, and say our own Jesus story, just as John stood on the shoulders of the synoptics, and told his own Jesus story. He shows how John selects and transforms pieces of the Gospels tradition, and invites followers now to run as those liberated from previous cultures, and discovering new incarnations, which in turn create new contextual practice, and consequent new presentations of the radical gospel.

3

Footwashing and Diaconal Ordination

LESLIE J. FRANCIS

Introduction

The aim of this chapter is to draw together two distinctive approaches to scripture (Practice Interpretation and the SIFT hermeneutical method) by designing a qualitative empirical study that invited experienced preachers to reflect on the footwashing account presented in John 13:2b-15 in the light of exhortation offered within the context of the Anglican ordination service to those about to be made deacon.

Practice interpretation of scripture, with its roots in the work of John Vincent, recognises, appreciates and promotes ways in which dialogue can be established between the text of scripture and the day-to-day practical issues faced by the churches (see, for example, Vincent, 2006). In the present study the practical issue concerns reflecting on the role of the deacon within contemporary Anglican churches and equipping newly ordained deacons to exercise an effective and fulfilling ministry. In the present study the text of scripture has been identified as the Johannine footwashing narrative in light of the long-established link between this narrative and diaconal ministry.

The SIFT hermeneutical method, with its roots in the work of Leslie J. Francis, takes seriously the "reader perspective" approaches to biblical interpretation and maintains that the reader perspective is influenced by the reader's psychological type preferences (see, for example, Francis &Village, 2008). Psychological type theory has its origins in the pioneering and creative work of Carl Jung (see, for example, Jung, 1971), and has been developed and clarified through measures like the Myers-Briggs Type Indicator (Myers & McCaulley, 1985) and the Francis Psychological Type Scales (Francis, 2005). At its heart psychological type theory distinguishes between two core psychological processes: the perceiving (or irrational) process concerned with data gathering, and the judging (or rational) process concerned with data evaluation.

According to this theory, each process is reflected in two opposing functions. In terms of perceiving, individuals show preferences either for sensing or for intuition. In terms of judging, individuals show preference either for thinking or for feeling. Moreover, for each individual either the preferred perceiving process (sensing or intuition) or the preferred judging process (thinking or feeling) takes precedence over the others, leading to clearly recognised dominant psychological types: dominant sensing, dominant intuition, dominant thinking, and dominant feeling.

In terms of the perceiving functions, sensing types focus on the realities of the situation as perceived by the senses. They tend to concentrate on specific details, rather than on the overall picture. They are concerned with the actual, the real, and the practical. They tend to be down-to-earth and matter-of-fact. Intuitive types focus on the possibilities of the situation, perceiving meanings and relationships. They tend to concentrate on associations, intuitions and on the wider themes that go well beyond the sense perceptions. They tend to focus on the bigger picture and on the future possibilities, rather than on specific facts and details.

In terms of the judging functions, feeling types form evaluations based on subjective personal and interpersonal values. They emphasise compassion and mercy. They are known for their tactfulness and for their desire for peace. They are more concerned to provide harmony than to adhere to abstract principles. Thinking types form evaluations based on objective, impersonal logic, they emphasise integrity and justice. They are known for their truthfulness and for their desire for fairness. They consider conforming to principles to be more important than cultivating harmony.

The SIFT method of biblical hermeneutics, as displayed by Francis and Atkins (2000, 2001, 2002), maintains that a rounded approach to biblical interpretation is achieved by bringing each of these four functions to the passage in turn. The first step addresses the sensing perspective (S) by approaching the text through the five human senses, by attending to the practical and factual details, and by getting in touch with the physical realities. The second step addresses the intuitive perspective (N) by approaching the text through the imagination, by drawing links, by identifying the big themes, and by exploring possibilities. The third step addresses the feeling perspective (F) by identifying with the fundamental human values, by getting inside the human experience, by exploring the relationships, and by experiencing what it is to be truly human. The fourth step addresses the thinking perspective (T) by examining the matters of truth raised by the biblical text, by reflecting rationally and critically on issues of principle, and by identifying the underlying theological issues.

The SIFT approach was developed initially on the basis of theoretical extrapolation from basic Jungian psychological principles. Subsequently the approach has been supported by evidence from a series of empirical studies, employing both quantitative (Village & Francis, 2005; Francis, Robbins, Village, 2009; Village, 2010) and qualitative methodologies (Francis, 2010, 2012a, 2012b; Francis & Jones, 2011). Typically in the qualitative studies, experienced preachers have been invited to work in type-alike groups in order to reflect on a specified passage of scripture and to propose how they would preach on the passage. Typically these studies have identified and illustrated the connection between psychological type preference and biblical interpretation. The present study builds on this tradition, drawing on the Johannine footwashing narrative.

Method

1. Procedure
The exercise was embedded in a programme conducted for experienced preachers (clergy and readers) concerned with an introduction to psychological type theory and to reader perspectives on hermeneutical theory. In this context time was given to working in type-alike groups.

2. Measure
Psychological type was assessed by the 126-item Form G (Anglicised) of the Myers-Briggs Type Indicator (Myers & McCaulley, 1985). Broad support for the reliability and validity of this instrument is provided in the international literature, as summarised by Francis and Jones (1999), who additionally demonstrated the psychometric properties of the instrument among a sample of 429 adult British churchgoers.

3. Sample
The sample comprised 11 women and 10 men. There were more introverts (15) than extraverts (6), more judgers (14) than perceivers (7), and more intuitives (12) than sensers (9), but roughly equal numbers of thinkers (11) and feelers (10). In terms of dominant types, there were 6 dominant feelers, 5 dominant thinkers, 5 dominant sensers, and 5 dominant intuitives.

Results

1. Dominant sensing

The dominant sensing groups focused very clearly on what the text actually said. They located the passage within the context of John's account of Jesus' last meal with his disciples. Then they were caught up sharply by the opening words "during supper". Liturgically they had been accustomed to envisage the footwashing *before* supper, but now they were challenged to see this take place during the supper itself. The liturgical sequencing made more sense than washing feet in the middle of the meal. Jesus moves away from the table; Jesus removes his outer robe and takes the towel; Jesus washes the disciples' feet and dries them; Jesus puts his robe back on and returns to the table. All of these actions display the theme of servanthood.

They listened carefully to the conversation and tried to make sense of it all. The conversation between Jesus and Peter showed that Peter meant well, but misunderstood what was going on. From his Jewish roots, Peter had his own misconceptions about cleanliness, and Jesus is trying to help Peter understand cleanliness in a different way. At first Peter refused to have his feet washed; then Peter asked for his hands and his feet to be washed. Peter continues to see things "up-side-down".

In the middle of all this Jesus addresses the one who is to betray him and says "Not all of you are clean". But the betrayer is not identified.

At the end of the passage Jesus explains what he is doing. Jesus calls himself "Lord and teacher", and says, "You didn't think that I (your Lord and teacher) would be doing this for you. But I did. So go and do likewise!"

Having so carefully revisited the details of the narrative, the dominant sensing group posed for themselves the question: What do we want to draw out from the passage? Jesus set his disciples an example. It is this example that the newly ordained deacons should follow. They should follow Jesus' example, and not the example given by other people in the church. Following Jesus' example means that you will be doing things that other people do not expect you to be doing and doing things that you do not expect yourself to be doing.

2. Dominant intuition

The dominant intuition group went directly to the big picture and to the major themes. They found four themes that were developed in interesting ways.

The first big-picture theme was stimulated by the image of Jesus taking off his robe and tying a towel around himself. This very action showed Jesus taking the place of the lowest slave. This group saw the whole of the doctrine of the incarnation summed up in this one sentence from John's account of the supper. The newly ordained deacon, too, is called to an incarnational ministry. Self-emptying is at the heart of incarnational ministry.

The second big-picture theme was stimulated by the image of Peter's struggle to accept Jesus washing his feet. Peter had to learn to receive as well as to give. Mutuality of caring is at the heart of the gospel. The newly ordained deacon is ordained not only to serve, but also to be open to being served by others. To accept the service of others is to lay aside pride and to embrace humility.

The third big-picture theme was stimulated by Jesus' proclamation, "And you are clean". We are washed clean when we are baptised, when we are baptised in the Spirit, when we are washed in the blood of the Lamb slain from the beginning. But do we stay clean? The newly ordained deacon is challenged to be alert to all that can tarnish and corrupt.

The fourth big-picture theme followed on from the third as a consequence of becoming attracted by the powerful image of water as the agent of cleansing. To do its job water too must not stagnate; water must keep moving and flowing. Grace flows like water, otherwise it too stagnates. The newly ordained deacon is called to serve as a conduit for God's grace. And Jesus set an example of that by the way in which he washed his disciples' feet. It is through such actions that the deacon may serve as a conduit of God's grace.

3. Dominant feeling

The dominant feeling group began by trying to place themselves in Jesus' shoes. The whole of this meal must have been so emotionally draining for Jesus. It was, in their words, a "bitter sweet" occasion. There was a sense of foreboding overhanging Jesus, a sense of melancholy as he looked back on his closest group of friends, knowing that one of them was about to betray him. There was also a sense of urgency as Jesus wanted to give his followers a lasting pattern to follow.

In this situation, Jesus took something very ordinary, very homely, and he transformed it into something extraordinary. Jesus took an ordinary basin and poured into it ordinary water. By the way he did this he changed the way his disciples saw him. By taking ordinary things, and by doing extraordinary things with them, the newly ordained deacon is called to change people's lives.

In this situation, Jesus took on a very ordinary role for himself. He replaced his outer robe with a towel. He took off his outer mantle as Lord and teacher and became the slave for others. By the ministry of service, the newly ordained deacon is called to change people's lives.

The dominant feeling group went on to place themselves in Peter's shoes. Peter felt affronted by Jesus' attempt to wash his feet. Peter was so self-sufficient, so sure of his call to serve others, that he could not face being served by Jesus. Peter could not endure the sense of vulnerability, the sense of humiliation that such an act would engender. Peter speaks out his resistance.

In this situation the penny at last drops for Peter. At last Peter experiences what it means to be a disciple and he surrenders his pride, he accepts his vulnerability and he accepts Jesus' invitation to him. The newly ordained deacon has been ordained not only to serve, but to accept the service of others within the Church.

In this Gospel passage two examples have been set: one by Jesus and one by Peter. The newly ordained deacon is called to learn from and to follow both examples.

4. Dominant thinking

The dominant thinking group set out to identify and to isolate the main theological issues suggested by the passage and came up with four different approaches.

They identified the first theological issue as concerned with "cleanliness and sanctification". Water, they recognised, is a central and core image within John's Gospel, perhaps even to the point of John giving more attention to the sacrament of baptism than to the sacrament of eucharist. Cleanliness and sanctification are core to the call to discipleship and to the call to ministry. Jesus' reference to the one who is not clean is a proper warning to us all. Even the newly ordained deacon cannot take things too much for granted. The deacon needs to maintain the ongoing relationship with Jesus. We need to let Jesus wash us and make us clean.

They identified the second theological issue as concerned with "models of leadership". The passage shows Jesus as claiming three models of leadership for himself. Jesus claims servant ministry, teacher ministry, and lordship ministry. Jesus is not claiming that his ministry as servant replaces, takes over from or supersedes his ministry as teacher and his ministry as Lord. In this passage, Jesus specifically affirms these models as much as he affirms the model of servant. The newly ordained deacon needs to embrace a diversity of ministry roles that should be complementary and held in tension.

They identified the third theological issue as concerned with "the concept of servanthood before Holy Eucharist". The passage shows Jesus laying down his outer robe as prefiguring laying down his life. This is the ultimate servanthood. Following Jesus' example can be costly for the newly ordained deacon.

They identified the fourth theological issue as concerned with "the idea of the servant leader". The dominant thinking group questioned the wisdom of the Church giving too much emphasis to the idea of servant leadership (a notion gaining ascendancy, it was argued, in some circles). The newly ordained deacon should not be capture by the false theology underpinning this notion. The deacon is not called to be a doormat; the deacon must be prepared to challenge people and to upset people. All this is as much part of the calling to diaconal ministry as the role of servant.

Conclusion

This study set out to test the application of the SIFT hermeneutical method for the practice interpretation of the Johannine footwashing narrative applied to the context of diaconal ordination. A sample of 21 experienced preachers worked within four type-alike groups separating out dominant sensing types, dominant intuitive types, dominant feeling types, and dominant thinking types. Working in type-alike groups these experienced preachers produced four distinctive reflections on and applications of the Johannine footwashing narrative consistent with the theoretical framework underpinning the SIFT hermeneutical method. The dominant sensing group focused very closely on what the text actually said. The dominant intuition group went directly to the big picture and to the major themes. The dominant feeling group began by placing themselves first in Jesus' shoes and then in Peter's shoes, savouring the narrative through the perspective of the key participants. The dominant thinking group set out to identify and to isolate the main theological themes suggested by the passage.

On the basis of these findings, the conclusion can be drawn that a richer and more fully nuanced practice interpretation of the Johannine footwashing narrative for the biblically-based illumination of the diaconal ministry can be achieved by approaching the text through the disciplined application of the four Jungian functions of sensing, intuition, feeling and thinking, as commended by the SIFT method of biblical hermeneutics and liturgical preaching.

Further studies are now needed to replicate this empirical hermeneutical enquiry based on the Johannine footwashing narrative among other groups of experienced preachers, in order to test the generalisability of implications for the practice interpretation of scripture.

Bibliography

Francis, L.J. (2005). *Faith and Psychology: Personality, Religion and the Individual,* London: Darton, Longman and Todd

—— (2010). "Five Loaves and Two Fishes: An Empirical Study in Psychological Type and Biblical Hermeneutics among Anglican Preachers". *HTS Theological Studies,* 66(1), art. 811, 1-5

—— (2012a). "What Happened to the Fig Tree? An Empirical Study in Psychological Type and Biblical Hermeneutics". *Mental Health, Religion and Culture, 15,* 873-891

—— (2012b). "Interpreting and Responding to the Johannine Feeding Narrative: An Empirical Study in the SIFT Hermeneutical Method among Anglican Ministry Training Candidates". *HTS Theological Studies, 68*(1), art. 1205, 1-9

—— & Jones, S.H. (2011). "Reading and Proclaiming the Resurrection: An Empirical Study in Psychological Type Theory among Trainee and Experienced Preachers Employing Mark 16 and Matthew 28". *Journal of Empirical Theology,* 24, 1-18

—— & Atkins, P. (2000). *Exploring Luke's Gospel: A Guide to the Gospel Radings in the Revised Common Lectionary.* London: Mowbray

—— & Atkins, P. (2001). *Exploring Matthew's Gospel: A Guide to the Gospel Readings in the Revised Common Lectionary.* London: Mowbray.

—— & Atkins, P. (2002). *Exploring Mark's Gospel: An Aid for Readers and Preachers Using Year B of the Revised Common Lectionary.* London: Continuum

—— & Jones, S.H. (1999). "The Scale Properties of the MBTI Form G (Anglicised) among Adult Churchgoers". *Pastoral Sciences* 18, 107-126

—— , Robbins, M., & Village, A. (2009). "Psychological Type and the Pulpit: An Empirical Enquiry Concerning Preachers and the SIFT Method of Biblical Hermeneutics". *HTS Theological Studies* 65(1), art. 161, 1-7

—— & Village, A. (2008). *Preaching with All Our Souls.* London: Continuum.

Jung, C.G. (1971). *Psychological Types: The Collected Works,* vol. 6. London: Routledge and Kegan Paul

Myers, I.B., & McCaulley, M.H. (1985). *Manual: A Guide to the Development and Use of the Myers-Briggs Type Indicator.* Palo Alto, CA: Consulting Psychologists Press

Village, A. (2010). "Psychological Type and Biblical Onterpretation among Anglican Clergy in the UK". *Journal of Empirical Theology* 23, 179-200

—— & Francis, L.J. (2005). "The Relationship of Psychological Type Preferences to Biblical Interpretation". *Journal of Empirical Theology* 18 (1), 74-89

Vincent, J.J. (2006). "Practice Interpretation". Pp. 29–32 in J. Vincent (ed.), *Mark, Gospel of Action: Personal and Community Responses* London: SPCK.

4

Sin, Righteousness and Judgment

DAVID BLATHERWICK

In John 16.8-11, Jesus tells his disciples that, after his death, resurrection and exaltation, the Spirit will show them that people's understanding of "sin", "righteousness" and "judgment" is wrong. They are wrong about sin, he says, because they do not believe in him, about righteousness, because he is going to the Father and his disciples will no longer see him, and about judgment, "because the ruler of this world has been condemned".

The context is Jesus' warning to his disciples that they will be banned from synagogues and attacked by people who think they are defending God's honour by killing them (16.1-4). Jesus tells them that he will send them the Spirit (16.7). The Spirit will convince them that he is right and they should go on trusting him (16.8-11; cf. 14.1-4). He will also say things that Jesus has not been able to say (16.12-14).

I assume that Jesus sees "sin", "righteousness" and "judgment" as the big issues in his debates with his critics – as they would be in the postmortems that went on in Jewish communities all over the Mediterranean world after Roman armies destroyed the temple in Jerusalem in 70 CE.

Jesus' debates with his critics about sin, in John's Gospel, focus on sin in the forms of failure to respect the Sabbath day and blasphemy – his claim to know God's mind because he is God's son (5.1-46; 9.1-41; 10.22-39).

His comments about judgment assume that his critics have already reached a decision about him, but do not realise that in doing so they have passed judgment on themselves (3.18-21, 36; 5.22-30; 8.15-51; 12.31, 44-50).

Jesus does not use the noun "righteousness" or "justice" elsewhere in John's Gospel, but does say that his judgment of people is "just" or "fair", unlike that of his critics (5.30; 7.24), and prays to God, his "just" or "righteous" Father (17.25).

There is, of course, a concept of righteousness in the Old Testament which is relevant to this discussion. It is seen in the story of Phinehas, who saves his people from God's wrath by driving a spear through a fellow Israelite and his Midianite lover (Numbers 25), in the demand that Israelites kill false prophets, messianic pretenders and all who try to lead them astray (Deuteronomy 13; 18.9-22) and in the procedure for stoning rebellious sons (Deuteronomy 21.18-21). We find it in the New Testament too – in Joseph's need to divorce Mary, because she is pregnant (Matthew 1.18), and the concern of scribes and Pharisees that people respect the Sabbath day, observe the rules of purity, pay tithes, practice piety, perform acts of mercy and, in general, stay true to God. Central to it is a conviction that a righteous person will always do whatever is necessary to defend God's honour and that of God's people – using violence sometimes – and to protect his or her own.

1. Jesus' Crucifixion

I do not think any of the people directly responsible for Jesus' death were in any doubt that what they were doing was right.

Pilate was determined to stamp out trouble – especially at Passover. There was no place for trouble-makers in Pilate's world. The punishment might seem harsh, but it was certainly effective. Law and order must be maintained – in the interests of Jews as well as Romans. Jesus' death would be a warning to others who might be planning demonstrations like his dramatic entry into Jerusalem or his protest in the temple. Crucifying criminals on Golgotha at Passover would be like showing executions on prime time television on Christmas Eve or before the Queen's Speech on Christmas Day. If it happened regularly, as the conversation about releasing a prisoner in Mark 15.6-15 seems to suggest, it would be intended to show people who was in charge and discourage displays of anti-Roman feeling during the festival. It would cast a long shadow over nearly everyone's celebrations.

In the first three Gospels, the chief priests, elders and scribes seem to have been reacting to what Jesus had been doing in the temple – in particular, his attempt to clear the space in which the animals needed for sacrifices were sold and ordinary coins exchanged for those used in the temple. (John places the incident earlier in his account of Jesus' life.) The temple lay at the heart of Israel's life, attracting Jews from all over the world, especially at festival times, to offer sacrifices and pray. No one could be allowed to obstruct them in doing that or put people's lives at risk with impromptu demonstrations. It is not clear which would have hurt more – Jesus' description of the temple as "a den of thieves" or his implied prophecy of its impending doom.

In John's Gospel, on the other hand, they seem to be under pressure from Pilate to have Jesus arrested and handed over to him. As those responsible for law and order in the city, they know they can either resist and see what happens or comply. Caiaphas has no doubt that they should comply. It would make no sense to put the nation's future at risk for the sake of one man – especially not for a man like Jesus (John 11.45-53). But if Pilate had wanted to get hold of the person who had staged a mock coronation parade and was causing such a stir, he seems to have decided quite quickly that he was not dangerous and could safely be released. But the chief priests, elders and scribes insisted that he be killed, so he had him killed. If he regretted anything later, it would probably be that he had let them hustle him. But then, in the give and take of politics, "You win some and you lose some!"

The crowd that clamoured for Jesus' blood outside Pilate's palace – as distinct from the one that had welcomed him into the city – may have been told things about him that disturbed them. He was in league with the devil and deceived people by magic. He intended to destroy the temple (also by magic?). He was lax in his observance of the Mosaic laws and happy for his followers to be lax in their observance too. He was leading people astray and needed to be killed. They might not have liked the idea of Barabbas being freed, but better a convicted killer at large in the city than Jesus!

The soldiers called upon to escort Jesus to Golgotha and execute him did what soldiers do – obeyed orders. They could have chosen not to add to his humiliation by mocking him, but they were obliged to carry out the court's sentence. It was not their job to question it and most of them would have assumed that the sentence was just or, if not just, necessary. The centurion was not so sure, As Jesus died, he said he was a son of God (Matt. 27.54; Mark 14.39) or, more simply, a righteous man (Luke 23.47). He was not questioning Pilate's right to execute troublemakers in that way, just the appropriateness of his decision in Jesus' case.

2. Time for Reflection?

But if the people responsible for putting Jesus to death were quite sure at the time that what they were doing was right, might they not have felt differently about it later?

Did Pilate ever doubt that the Romans were destined by the gods to rule the world, to bring peace where there had been war, order where there had been chaos and a new prosperity that would carry all of humanity into a new Golden Age? That Roman rule could best be described as "firm but fair" and that the punishments meted out to wrongdoers were appropriate to their crimes? That some nations were born to rule and others to be ruled? Did he doubt that it was in everyone's interest that the smallholdings of simple farmers should be absorbed into the larger units farmed by the rich and that Jews should be taxed heavily to pay for the benefits of Roman rule? I do not think so. He would certainly not have seen himself as a thief or robber who had entered the sheepfold by climbing over a wall or a wolf who was savaging the sheep (John 10.7-14). Leaders or representatives of powerful nations rarely see their interference in other nations' affairs in such terms!

Similarly, Luke does not give the impression that the chief priests, elders and scribes had any misgivings about what they had done. They would not have seen themselves as hirelings – men who cared more for themselves and their comfortable lifestyles than for their sheep (John 10.12-13). When Peter accused them of betraying a righteous man – and not merely handing him over to Pilate but badgering Pilate to crucify him, when he seemed likely to let him go – they were not prepared to listen. They ordered him and the other apostles to be quiet (Acts 3.17; 4.16-22). When they refused, they would have sentenced them to death, had not Gamaliel intervened (5.17-39). They did sentence Stephen to death (7.54-60), the high priest authorised Paul's mission to Damascus (9.1-2) and, later, some of them clearly wanted Paul himself killed, when the tribune responsible for keeping order in the temple brought him before them for preliminary examination (23.6-10).

Luke notes that the high priest was supported by the Sadducees in his efforts to silence Peter and the other apostles, but not by Gamaliel, the Pharisee (Acts 5.17-39; cf. also 23.6-10). Even so, there were Pharisees, like Gamaliel's student Paul, who were prepared to do almost anything to stop the new movement taking root (Acts 8.1; 9.1-2; cf. Gal. 1.13-14; Phil. 3.4-5). Following the destruction of the temple, attitudes seem to have hardened. Leading Pharisees pinned the blame for the tragedy, not on a few hot-heads (as Josephus did), but on all those Jews who had been lax in their observance of God's laws and not lived up to his expectations of them.

Some of the people in the crowds that had shouted for Jesus' blood outside Pilate's palace or mocked him as he died may have regretted it later. But they were not the first people to be stirred to anger in a crowd and would not be the last (cf. Acts 6.12-15; 14.19-20; 17.5-9,14; 21.27-36). Priests and politicians are past masters in the art of stirring people up by playing on their ignorance or fear and large crowds of people are notoriously unpredictable and occasionally very violent.

But does John's Jesus expect anything much to change as a result of his death or the work of the Spirit? I doubt it. The optimism we find at the end of Matthew's Gospel and Luke's is singularly lacking at the end of John's. In Matt. 28.18-20, Jesus claims authority over everything and tells his disciples to "make disciples of all nations". In Luke 24.44-49, he tells them to wait in Jerusalem until they are "clothed with power from on high" and then to do the same (cf. Acts 1.8). But, in John 21.13-19, all he asks Peter to do is look after his sheep and prepare himself for martyrdom.

3. John 16.8-11 in its Context

The tragedy of Jesus' life, according to this Gospel, is that God sends his son into the world to save, not judge it (3.17), and he is greeted with either hostility or indifference. The only people to welcome him are those whose deeds are true and clearly done in God (3.21; cf. Matthew 5.16), who only want to do God's will, with no concern for their own reputations (7.17; cf. 12.43) or are, like Nathaniel, without guile (1.47). Jesus is sent into the world to save it, but soon realises that that is impossible. So he concentrates on helping those who are prepared to listen to him and trust him to escape (3.16) – and on leaving an unforgettable image of total obedience to God behind him (3.14).

The people who reject or ignore him are doing what people have done from the beginning of time. As the creative Word, he created a world full of life and light and has had to fight the forces of darkness from day one (1.3-5). He is the light inside every human being, urging us to grow, to learn and to reach out towards God's future, but we resist him (1.10). He made a home for himself among a people he thought he could work with, but they did not want to know him either (1.11). But there have always been some people prepared to share his dreams and become children of God (1.12).

Jesus invites people into another world that only those who are born of water and of Spirit can know (3.3-7). He speaks of himself as a ladder reaching up to heaven, with angels going up and down it (1.51) and describes how God will lift him up on a cross to show everyone that "the ruler of this world" has no power over him (3.14-15; cf. 12.31; 16.33), or over those who believe in him. He also speaks of an imminent judgment, involving both the living and the dead, that those who believe in him need not fear, because they will pass straight through death into life (5.19-29).

Jesus' critics are mainly concerned about this world – their land, their temple and their way of life. They are determined to defend God's honour and draw strength from observing Moses' laws – laws given to them by God, that do not need to be supplemented by anything that Jesus brings (cf. 1.17). God has given them a land to live in. It is theirs to enjoy, protect and keep holy, as far as they can in the present circumstances. They do not long for another home, as Jesus does, but concentrate on being true to God in the here and now. Dreams of heaven are a luxury they cannot afford.

The mistake that they and many others make is, in Jesus' estimation, to reject or ignore him. As he says to Nicodemus, quite early in the story:

> This is the judgement [*sic*], that the light has come into the world, and people loved darkness rather than light because their deeds were evil (3.19; cf. 1.4-9).

The mistake Nicodemus and his colleagues make is to realise that Jesus is a teacher who has come from God and not to act on what he says. Nicodemus does not understand what Jesus means by being born of the Spirit, or born from above (3.3-6), and does not relish the idea of being blown about by the Spirit, like a leaf in the wind (3.8). He likes to keep his feet firmly on the ground and is prepared to stand up for Jesus, at some risk to himself (7.50-52), or, with Joseph of Arimathea, bury him (19.32), but not to burn his boats and join him (cf. 6.66-71; 12.37-43).

The mistake Jesus' disciples can make is to lose their faith in him, to allow themselves to be frightened by the Evil One or to fall into one of his traps. They must support one another (13.34-35) and present a united front to the world (17.20-21). The world will hate them, as it has hated him and as it hates God (15.18-25). The Spirit will, with their help, bear witness to the world's hatred of him (15.26-27), but the world is unlikely to take any notice, because "it neither sees him nor knows him" (14.17). The disciples can bear witness to the world more effectively by keeping their distance from it than by preaching to it or trying to engage with it (17.6-26). They will need to have the courage of their convictions (14.1-4), the same calmness and steely resolve in the face of danger that Jesus has (14.27) and be ready to die for God, when the time comes, as Jesus is (17.1-5).

Jesus' parting message to his disciples is, according to the author of 1 John:

> Do not love the world or the things in the world. The love of the Father is not in those who love the world, for all that is in the world – the desire of the flesh, the desire of the eyes, the pride in riches – comes not from the Father but from the world. And the world and its dreams are passing away, but those who do the will of God live for ever (1 John 2.15-17).

That is, the world and everything in it was made by God, through Jesus, but has become so warped or perverted that anyone who wants to give his/her allegiance to God needs to be weaned from it.

As someone who looks first to Mark's Gospel and then to Matthew's and Luke's for his idea of Jesus, I find John's picture of him disconcerting. He seems to be remarkably unconcerned about the world's fate and does not try to avert it, even refusing to pray for it in his final prayer

(17.9). He does not tell his disciples to love their enemies or pray for them, as he does in Matt. 5.43-48, and describes the commandment to love one another as "new" (13.34), as if it adds something to the two great commandments of Jewish tradition rather than subtracts from them. He seems to use miracles to make theological points rather than to help people, using the healing of a man on the Sabbath, for example, to assert his right to work when God works (5.2-9) and the healing of a blind man to show that he is the light of the world (9.1-7). He allows Lazarus to die, so that Martha will see him as the resurrection and the life and he can tell everyone that they will not die, if they believe in him (11.1-53). He talks to a Samaritan woman about the water he can give her that will gush up, like a spring, inside her (4.7-15; cf. 7.37-40) and feeds a crowd of people by the lakeside so that he can talk about the true bread from heaven, his body, that, with his blood, will give them eternal life (6.35-65) – not because they are hungry.

The world, he says to his disciples, will soon be gone. In the meantime, they will experience all the horrors of living in a world that hates them. He cannot ask God to take them out of the world, but can ask him to give them strength (17.6-26). There will be times when they are strongly tempted to make their peace with the world simply to survive, but they must resist the temptation. He will be preparing homes for them in his Father's house and that is where he wants them to be (14.1-4).

In Conclusion

We would like to think that the world has moved on since Jesus' time and that the barbarism evident in the stories of Jesus' death is no longer with us and that rich or powerful people no longer use threats of violence or victimisation to stifle criticism. We would also like to think that we have, as followers of Jesus, looked closely at our use of words like "sin", "righteousness" and "judgment", to make sure that we use them positively, to help and encourage people, to strengthen and embolden them, rather than negatively, to keep them in line or control them.

The great sin, according to Jesus in John's Gospel, is to refuse to trust him, to be so rooted in the here and now, or in the past, that we turn down God's invitation to become his children and live, as Abraham, Isaac, Moses and others lived, for a transformed world (Heb. 11.1–12.2). It is to be unwilling to let the Spirit make us the mature people God wants us to be. In general, Jesus sees sin as not doing what God wants rather than not obeying his laws, doing things for our own glory rather than his or passing our deeds off as genuine when they are not. A righteous person is prepared to do anything to make people aware of God's blessing, like Abraham, but does not see extreme violence as one of the tools. He/she knows that God loved the world so much that he sent

Jesus into it to save it, but the world killed him and cut itself off from the source of its life. What is about to happen to it will not be the act of a vengeful God, who will stop at nothing to punish those who refuse to live by his rules, but a tragedy he tried to avert but could not.

Select Bibliography

Philo, *Life of Moses*, Philo VI, Loeb Classical Library, London: Heinemann; Cambridge, MA: Harvard University Press, 1959

Josephus, *New Complete Works*, Grand Rapids, MI: Kregel Academic, 1999

Barrett, C. Kingsley, *The Gospel According to St. John*, 2nd ed., London: SPCK, 1978

Daube, David, *Collaboration with Tyranny in Rabbinic Law*, London: Oxford University Press, 1965

Lau, Rabbi Binyamin, *The Sages: Character, Context and Creativity*, vol. 2, Jerusalem: Maggid Books, Koren Publishers, 2001

Martyn, J. Louis, *History and Theology in the Fourth Gospel*, 3rd ed., Louisville, KY: Westminster John Knox Press, 2003.

5

Friendship in John 15: In the Legal Workplace

SARAH PULLIN

I have worked as a lawyer for over 20 years in a variety of types and sizes of firms, and am currently in a large multinational. I have also recently become an ordained Anglican priest with the focus of ministry in the business and workplace. Like many, I live with the restrictions that practicing an all-consuming professional career imposes on life – and yet there is a constant pull and desire to connect with God and the church that never wains. I have observed over the years that this apparent dichotomy can often lead to increasing tensions between the two or even the giving up of one – leaving the career or increasingly disconnecting with God. I suggest John 15 helps to provide an answer to this impasse. Based on a discourse analysis of Jesus' witness to friendship in John 15, this article explores the practice of Christian friendship in the legal workplace. It demonstrates that friendship has the potential to contribute to mission and discipleship in a business context.

1. Discourse Analysis

A new commandment	The prayer of Jesus
Chapter 13	Chapter 17
Jesus the way and	Jesus' departure and
the Holy Spirit	the Holy Spirit
Chapter 14	Chapter 16
Friendship	
Chapter 15	

Chapter 15's location in the Farewell Discourse

My discourse analysis of John 15 follows the method put forward by Holgate and Starr (2006: 48-54). Having first acknowledged the context of John 15 within John's Farewell Discourse and John as a whole, including his Prologue, my analysis draws our attention to some important features of John's presentation of Jesus' understanding of friendship.

The first feature is that first friendship is central to Jesus' relationship with the disciples. Second, Jesus' friendship with the disciples is set within the context of them having been called, chosen and appointed. Third, the disciples' friendship with Jesus is central to understanding the disciples' relationship with the Father and the world, and fourth friendship is sustained by abiding.

Consequences of the Father's actions
Verses 1-4

Consequences of the Spirit's actions
Verses 26–(16:)4a

Consequences of the disciples' actions
Verses 5-8

Consequences of the world's actions
Verses 21-25

Consequences of Jesus' and the
disciples' actions
Verses 9-13

Consequences of Jesus' and the
world's actions
Verses 17 - 20

Consequences of Jesus calling, choosing
and appointing – friendship
Verses 14-16

The structural features of John 15

The main verbs in this chapter highlight the equal importance of being *chosen* along with *abiding*, *hate* and *love*. It is the semantic domain *chosen*, *called* and *appointed*, that makes up the greatest emphasis of action of the main verbs in the text. Interestingly, taking the text as a whole there is the same number of occurrences of *testify* as there are *bear*, indicating proactive as well as consequential outcomes to being chosen, called and appointed.

A progression is noted through the text of the changing emphasis in the use of the main verbs: *abide* appears in the first half of the text; *chosen*, *called* and *appointed* are concentrated around the middle; *love* appears either side of the middle portion of the text; and *hate* is in the second half of the text. The dualistic nature of John is often highlighted, here in the text love and hate. The analysis of the main verbs in the text suggests that it is perhaps premature to look at the dualistic nature of the text before recognising the overall structure and progression through it. In other words one might miss that love and hate are the consequential actions towards those who have been chosen, called and appointed as opposed to inherent characteristics of groups of people. This progression is also seen grammatically by the changes in verb tenses used, from past through to present and then future, as well as also being reflected in the narrative story.

However, most of the verbs used in the text are not the main verbs but nominal, adjectival or adverbial verbs used in dependent subclauses. The most common verb used in the dependent subclauses is *abide*. The main verbs should be understood then in the light of *abide* rather than abide being understood as an end in itself. Likewise "*love* one another ..." (v. 12) is a dependent subclause which should be understood in the light of command, the prerequisite to being friends (vv. 14-16).

When the text is split into cola, my analysis suggests this is a pattern that continues through the whole text, creating seven small units. The appreciation of seven small units highlights a central fourth unit, verses 14 to 16, in which friendship is embedded and where it acts as the pivot between the internal and external worlds of disciples. The structure of John 15 made evident by this discourse analysis does not explain the meaning of friendship, but the context and place of friendship in the life of the disciples. It is friendship's pivotal position in the context of the progression through the text, its place between the resulting love and hate, and the importance of the activity of abiding that this analysis shows to be important.

Therefore the structure of John 15 suggests first that friendship has an impact inwards as well as outwards – inwards within the close relationships between the Father and the Son, and Jesus and the disciples, and outwards in the relationships of Jesus and the disciples in the world. Second, friendship exists temporally and atemporally – within the Trinity outside of time and through time; and vertically between "heaven" and horizontally on earth – highlighting Jesus' pivotal role to the world and also the disciples' role in following Jesus' example. Third, friendship operates across relationships and communities – the Trinity, the Church and the world. Fourth, the analysis points to the importance of being chosen and testifying for friendship: friendship is not only to be a characteristic of the Church-in-discipleship, but also a characteristic of the Church-in-mission in response to having been chosen, called and appointed. Therefore Christians should acknowledge the potential of friendship in the world and seek to demonstrate its potential.

2. The Potential of Christian Friendship in the World

This discourse analysis of John 15 shows Jesus' witness to friendship and demonstrates that the context of such friendship is both the Church and the Church in the world. What then is the potential of this Christian friendship in the world and, specifically, the workplace? How might Christian friendship be practised in the workplace? Friendship in the workplace as a general concept is already acknowledged as being highly relevant (Shellenbarger 2000). It is specifically relevant to the legal workplace because of the needs in this context and the life of a lawyer (www.thelawyer.com, LawCare 2011). Current Christian thought also notes friendship is particularly relevant today and there has been a surge in writings on friendship within different categories – feminism, ageism, disabilities and same-sex relationships (e.g. McFague 1983, 1987; Hauerwas 1998, 2000, 2000; Hauerwas & Wells 2006). Why then has there not been more Christian exploration of the practice of friendship in the workplace?

The answer is perhaps best arrived at by first acknowledging and then considering some of the hindrances that might be encountered in accepting friendship as a practice in the workplace - from a workplace perspective and from a Christian perspective. Some recognised common hindrances to accepting friendship as a practice that will be considered are over-particularisation, favourtism, staff turnover, the ability to form friendship at work and the place of egoism and altruism (Zaleznik 1997; Berman, et al. 2002; Shellenbarger 2000; Mao 2006). After considering the hindrances attention will then be given to the positive potential of friendship in the legal workplace through the formation, function and growth or deterioration of friendships – the particular nuanced aspects of friendship identified as being important in the workplace (Myers 2009).

Hindrances
The first hindrance is the over-particularisation of friendship and while this is a risk in any friendship research highlights this as having particularly detrimental effects in the workplace (Zaleznik 1997; Berman et al. 2002). In addition in the legal workplace, the difficulty of over-particularisation might occur across several friendships within a legal team; such that it is not so much a single friendship, but a collection of friendships which become over-particularised and exclusive. Also from a Christian perspective, Carmichael (2004:198) makes the point that in trying to address over-particularisation, the Christian risks losing the value of friendship as a practice altogether.

Carmichael suggests the Christian's response to over-particularisation should not be to veer away from friendship, but to embrace it. Carmichael shows that the affirmation of the other in friendship need not lead to over-particularisation when understood not as the prerequisite to forming friendships, but rather as that which friendship itself creates (Carmichael 2004:197). This interest in the other would care about the lawyer for their sake, for God, for the sake of the legal community and also for the self – the focus is on the other, and what they might become in friendship in the context of the legal community, not on what the other lawyer possesses prior to friendship (Carmichael 2004:198). This approach to friendship is very counter-cultural in a context where what a lawyer possesses is highly valued. Importantly the significance of self is also still acknowledged, the self also being vulnerable in the legal working world. Some might suggest this approach overly waters down friendship's particularism such that it is no longer friendship at all. This suggestion does not fully appreciate the more reserved external appearance of friendship between professionals and within a legal workplace (Richards 2002). Nor perhaps the ability and importance to hold together at the same time particular friendships that have formed which bear the fruit of acknowledging goodness in the other as the outcome of those relationships and friendships that do not require particularism at the formation stage. Such an approach also enables Christian lawyers to practice the values underlying Christian friendship in a non-Christian context where friendships might otherwise be difficult due to the absence of a common Christian basis.

Part of the issue with over-particularism is favouritism (Zaleznik 1997, Berman et al. 2002). In the legal workplace this would be of particular concern in management or supervision scenarios, especially as these relationships affect the allocation of work, utilisation rates, promotion and any disciplinary matters. Again friendship itself is not the issue, but either over-particularisation or an incomplete understanding of friendship where it is viewed as restricting objectivity between friends. French highlights the importance of "frankness of speech", *parrhesia,* in friendships in the workplace such that friendship is "robust not fragile" and permits friends "to say what they think" (French, 2007:267). Being able to manage others well where the values of the individual and the business can be held together should be a characteristic of Christian friendships in the workplace, not a reason not to form them, where perhaps other friendship might break down.

The impact of staff turnover on friendships (Shellenberger 2000) perhaps overlooks that friendships do not have to end at the point a lawyer leaves a particular place of work. The Christian can demonstrate this by the time the Christian continues to invest in the friendship after the person has left. This is particularly relevant to the legal workplace because of the emphasis on networks, but also because the recent recession has caused a significant level of lawyer turnover. In these circumstances the Christian's response is an important role model of friendship between the Christian and the lawyer who leaves, but also as role model for those who remain in the legal workplace. The impact of staff turnover is likely to be more significant when there is also over-particularisation of friendship, emphasising the importance of addressing both hindrances.

Workplace friendships have also been shown to decrease at higher organisational levels (Mao 2006). The issue of friendship being limited to the lower levels in the legal workplace will not only lead to isolation of more senior staff and managers, but will also mean that they are not able to access the benefits of friendship. This issue for senior staff and managers is also exacerbated by the lack of opportunity to create friendships at this level and therefore the prevalence of friendship. Again this perhaps is not a reason to reject friendship as a value in the workplace, but a reason to ensure opportunity for all, and the potential of friendship are demonstrated. This is not only because friendships will help create a more supportive environment, but because the lack of friendships has had a consequential negative effect on lawyers (www.thelawyer.com), for example stress, depression and addiction. Confidential counselling services and health and wellbeing initiatives specifically for lawyers, deal effectively with these effects on all levels in the legal workplace. 2010/11 statistics from one such counselling service indicated 74% of calls from lawyers related to the effects of stress, 12% to clinical depression, 7% to addictions. There has been a sevenfold increase in the use of this service and therefore the negative effects of the legal workplace on lawyers over a 12-year period (LawCare 2011). There clearly is an important need being addressed through these services, but friendship as a value in the legal workplace seeks to act preventatively to avoid these effects in the first place.

From a Christian perspective, another hindrance to the recognition of friendship as a value in the workplace is the dynamic between egoism and altruism. The Christian's view of the workplace is perhaps that egotistical values are those nurtured and required and that altruism has little place unless as part of corporate social responsibility initiatives. Is this well founded though? Research in the field of psychology by Schwartz (1992) has shown that people can relate to each other either as neighbours or as opponents (cf. John 15.15, "I do not call you servants any longer ... but I have called you friends."). These relationships emphasise values that are either self-deferential/altruistic concerned with the wellbeing of others, or that are self-referential/egotistic based on the pursuit of personal status and success (Schwartz 1992). The friendship value is within the self-transcendence benevolence group.

Integrating theories from psychology and leadership suggest that certain combinations of values can lead to effective leadership practices, which in turn lead to highly developed and effective teams. Interestingly, these are teams that are likely to contribute positively to outcomes and organisational objectives (Schwartz 1992; Bass 1985). This research emphasises that friendship is not inconsistent with the development of highly effective teams or leadership in business. It also shows that the values of power and achievement are not required for the development of such effective teams.

It should also be noted from this research that self-referential values and self-deferential values are not completely incompatible; there are certain values within these that can co-exist. This ability to have coexisting opposing values is important in the legal workplace and business context, because it affirms the traditional Christian concern for self-deferential values while affirming the lawyer's need to demonstrate competence, intelligence, independence of thought, and to control risk and progress, all of which are self-referential values.

So how does Christian friendship in the legal workplace hold egoism and altruism together? Aquinas demonstrates we love friends with the love of friendship because we want them to experience good for their own sake, but also because of the good we derive from them (Aquinas). This approach acknowledges the need for love of self as well as love of the other, the need for egoism and altruism such that they are not mutually exclusive. The need for love of self is also crucial for lawyers. In order to "survive" the context and all that is required, the lawyer must care for the self and seek to avoid the negative effects of the context. The Christian should model the compatibility of egoism and altruism, with care of self as an important characteristic.

Finally, before moving on to consider the positive aspects of the witness to Christian friendship in the workplace, it is worth noting that our discourse analysis of John 15 sets the practice of friendship within the practice of *abiding*. It is therefore necessary for a Christian understanding of friendship to explore *what abiding looks like when the Christian is in the world and specifically the workplace.* Christians are often isolated from other Christians in their places of work. But there are simple solutions that perhaps can help with this, for example the formation of a "hub" to connect Christians in their workplace spheres and across companies can provide opportunity to encourage "abiding". Providing opportunities to "abide" that fit and are appropriate to the workplace is also important, such as arranging virtual prayer at certain times of day, or prayer walking when buying a lunchtime sandwich, or meditating on a single verse through the day. These examples of how abiding might be practised in the workplace could also encourage the local church to value and support the ministry of Christians both in their local churches and in the contexts they find themselves in during the week. Work needs to be seen as a core Christian practice.

Potential

Having considered the hindrances to friendship as a practice in the legal workplace, consideration is now given to the positive contribution that Christian understandings of friendship can make to the formation, function and determination of friendships in the workplace.

The opportunity to form friendships was highlighted in organisational socialisation research by Myers (2009) as being important in the workplace. In the legal workplace, it is particularly difficult to form friendships because of the long working hours that restrict the creation of friendships outside of work, and the practice of autonomous working. This is important because of the typical character traits of lawyers: legal management research by Richards (Richards 2002) indicates that they are 75% more autonomous than the general public and 74% less sociable. Therefore the Christian's response to friendship in this context should be to encourage and create opportunities for friendship as well as demonstrate openness in the way Christians relate to individuals and those outside of their team.

As already noted, Mao's research (2006) showed that senior people have fewer opportunities to form friendships. In the legal workplace the ratio of heads of department and executive board members to other colleagues could be as low as 1:100. Therefore the Christian at this level should be particularly conscious of encouraging and creating opportunities for senior people in a firm to form friendships, internally or externally.

The legal workplace is also particularly hierarchical. The Christian in the legal context should ensure friendship can be formed at all levels not just some, as well as demonstrating friendships across these levels (Aquinas). Examples of opportunity within a level might be arranging informal discussions around coffee or breakfast to discuss the law, ensuring this is not for juniors but those at senior levels too. Both of these suggestions are sympathetic to the legal context: the recognition of the importance of peer-learning and apprentice-style learning for lawyers. But at the same time it has created opportunities for lawyers to form friendships and engender a sense of community which is also of benefit to the firm and where the community enables lawyers to feel they "belong". Opportunities across levels might include team events and activities where all roles participate and are valued, for instance establishing an internal choir or a social event for the whole practice.

Friendships can also occur through the organisational and management structures that are already in place. Where opportunities for friendship arise through the organisational structure, an understanding of friendship as growing over time is important (Wadell 2010:270) particularly when one remembers that lawyers do not tend to form friendships quickly (Richards 2002). Practising patience and commitment over time is counter-cultural and an important aspect of friendship in the legal workplace. Friendships formed within the organisation might be the only friendship opportunities available to some lawyers because of financial targets, autonomous working and demanding workloads. Such structures are also likely at times to bring people into contact with those they would not normally form friendships with. An understanding that friendship creates affirmation of the other and that reciprocity is returned by God, not the other (Aquinas), enables the Christian to genuinely demonstrate friendship where this might not otherwise be possible. This extends opportunities for friendship with others with whom there is no precondition of "attraction" to their character or personality.

The function of team in the workplace is often orientated towards tasks. It is important for the Christian in a legal team to recognise and encourage the function of a team as being one not solely restricted to task and outcome orientation; that the function of legal teams can be greater than this, i.e. for the whole community, for the team, task and individual.

The all-round wellbeing of the people in the legal context is also important. Therefore Christian friendships should exhibit concern for the wellbeing of fellow lawyers, their basic needs, safety and the recognition of existing relationships. It is important to note that the practice of friendship does not negate a political response from the Christian to the legal working context. For the Christian lawyer this is showing a concern for the terms of working within a particular firm, but also wider than this for the profession as a whole and its role in society through representative bodies and the Law Society nationally and locally.

Friendship in John 15 is marked by the knowledge of "secrets" which Jesus made known. In the legal context, where intellect is a valued commodity, Christian friendships should also demonstrate the value of wisdom. Wisdom can be differentiated from intellect and demonstrated at all levels. This again is an important point in the legal context where knowledge is paramount and is associated with competitive advantage. But Christians can point to true knowledge within their friendships, away from purely consequentialist outcomes, to knowledge of Jesus and the Father and the Trinitarian relationship, i.e. to wisdom that comes from God.

In addition to wisdom and knowledge, Christian friendship should also function to direct others towards goodness (Carmichael 2004). There are factors associated with the lawyer's role, for example competiveness and survival in a recessive economic climate, which mean friendships at times could be directed at anything other than goodness. At such times, Christians in the legal context can demonstrate friendship as a value that directs others towards goodness.

The potential for deterioration of friendships (Shellenbarger 2000) in the legal context is inevitable given that people change jobs, some people get promoted and there is in some firms an "up or out" culture. The legal context is also susceptible to the economic climate where redundancies are a response to this. It is important then that the Christian can understand friendships within this context and can demonstrate depth within them where otherwise they might come across as temporary or superficial. Aquinas' approach is helpful here as it recognises friendships can be temporary or long term and that Christians can practice both (Aquinas) and not be compromised.

3. Conclusion

The view of friendship developed from our discourse analysis of John 15 requires not only a revised understanding of friendship, but also a paradigm shift in the whole disposition of the Christian towards friendship in the world and the workplace. It not only requires a change in our understanding of friendship, but also in how we practise it. Friendship then is a key practice of the church. As Ford suggests, it is "intrinsic to Christian faith that it is true to itself only by becoming freshly embodied in different contexts". Therefore Christian friendship requires "necessary improvisations, new articulations and practices" for the workplace today (Ford 1999:139, 144).

Bibliography

Aquinas, T. *Summa Theologica* literally translated by Fathers of the English Dominican Province, 3 vols. (London: Burns & Oates, 1947; 1st ed. 1911, 2nd ed. rev. 1922)

Bass, B.M. (1985) *Leadership and Performance beyond Expectations*, New York: The Free Press

Berman, E.M., West, J.P., & Richter, N.M. (2002) "Workplace Relations: Friendship Patterns and Consequences (according to Managers)", *Public Administration Review* 62(2), pp. 217-230

Carmichael, L. (2004) *Friendship: Interpreting Christian Love*, London: Continuum International Publishing Group

French, R. (2007) "Friendship and organization: Learning from the western friendship tradition", *Management and Organisational History*, vol. 2, pp. 255-272

Ford, D.F. (1999) *Cambridge Studies in Christian Doctrine: Self and Salvation – Being Transformed*, Cambridge: Cambridge University Press

Hauerwas, S. (1998) *Sanctify Them in the Truth*, Nashville: Abingdon Press

—— (2000) *A Better Hope: Resources for a Church Confronting Capitalism, Democracy, and Postmodernity*, Grand Rapids: Brazos Press

—— and Wells, S. (eds.) (2006) *The Blackwell Companion to Christian Ethics*, Oxford: Blackwell Publishing

Holgate, D. Starr, R. (2006) *SCM Study Guide – Biblical Hermeneutics*, London: Hymns Ancient and Modern Ltd.

LawCare (2011) *2010/11 LawCare Statistics*, Unpublished letter to author: LawCare

Lawyer, The (2010) *Focus: Magic Circle work-life balance – work, rest and fair play*, [Online], available: http://www.thelawyer.com/focus-magic-circle-work-life-balance-work-rest-and-fair-play/1005127.article [Accessed: 09 April, 12]

Mao, H-Y. (2006) "The Relationship between Organizational Level and Workplace Friendship", *The International Journal of Human Resource Management* 17(10), pp. 1819-1833

Marelich, W. (1996) "Can we be friends?", *HR Focus* 73(8), pp. 17-18

McFague, S. (1983) *Metaphorical Theology: Models of God in Religious Language*, London: SCM

—— (1987) *Models of God: Theology for a Ecological Nuclear Age*, London: SCM

Myers, K.K. (2009) "Workplace Relationships and Member Negotiation", in Smith, S. & Wilson, S. (eds.) *New Directions in Interpersonal Communication Research*, Thousand Oaks: Sage

Richard, L (2002) "Herding Cats: The Lawyer Personality Revealed", *Report to Legal Management* 29, no.11, August 2002, pp. 2-11

Schwartz, S.H. (1992) "Universals in the Content and Structure of Values: Theoretical Advances and Empirical Tests in 20 Countries", in M.P. Zanna, M.P. (ed.) *Advances in Experimental Social Psychology* 25, Orlando: Academic Press, pp. 1-65

Shellenbarger, S. (2000) "An Overlooked Toll of Job Upheavals: Valuable Friendships", *Wall Street Journal* (Eastern ed.), January 12th, New York, B1

Zaleznik, A. (1997) "Real work", *Harvard Business Review* 75(6), 53-62.

Note

My thanks to David Holgate, principal of STETS and my MA supervisor.

6

Judas, the Common Purse and the Poor

DAVID McLOUGHLIN

In two places John's Gospel refers to Judas' role as the keeper of the common purse or box, *glossokomon* (John 12.6; 13.29) In both cases this is linked to providing for the poor, *ptochoi*. What I would like to do with you today is muse a little on this common fund and the poor and try and give it a wider potential contextual horizon of interpretation.

In John's Gospel this fund is linked to Judas's untrustworthiness and acquisitiveness, whereas elsewhere in the Synoptics, as in Mark, there is no reference to the fund, only that Judas is the "one who handed him over" which also appears in John 6.64, 71. Matt 26.14-16 does not mention the treasurer's role but does emphasise Judas asked for money to hand Jesus over although the motive for this is not clear and the 30 pieces of silver seem unknown to John. Luke characterises the act of betrayal as satanic possession in Luke 22.3-6. And John repeats this in 13.27, ending the section with "And it was night." with all the implications that light and darkness has in John and in anticipation of the glory that is about to be revealed. So there is a lot of interesting editing and shaping of fundamental sections of the tradition going on in these texts.

In the anointing incident in John 6 we have the two contrasting figures of Mary, who acts out of love and the insight of loving faith, i.e. she knows the significance of the one in their midst and reverences him, and of Judas who cannot accept this and becomes the figure of lack of faith, or at least the one most resistant to the way the gospel is opening up. Instead he appeals to the simpler thrust of the ministry, the care of the destitute, at which point John has Jesus allude to Deut. 15.11 "The needy will never be lacking in the land" – implying the rest of the text, "That is why I command you to open your hand to your poor and needy" (cf. Schnackenburg, 1980, vol. 2, pp. 365-373). They can always work with the poor whereas he will not always be with them. There are two levels being played on here in John. Mary has engaged with the higher; Judas can't or won't see it.

But let's return to the common purse. What is the cultural context for this common fund?

According to Malina and Rohrbaugh (1998) the *glossokomon*, which the NRSV translates as "common purse", was a "coin case or box adopted as a security arrangement by Jerusalem pilgrims for transporting temple redemption money, taxes and alms." But they give no sources for this. There are two references to glossokomon in the LXX, one in 2 Chron. 24.8-10 and one in 2 Kings 12. In both cases these are boxes constructed to receive temple offerings not for the poor but for the rebuilding of the temple.

The two references in John to the common purse and the giving of alms to the *ptochoi* are within the context of Bethany and Jerusalem (12.5-8; 13.29). I will return to the location and its possible significance later. So the text implies Jesus and his group give alms and they have a common purse. In the history of interpreting this text there is a clear line of interpretation in Brown (*John XIII–XXI*, p. 576) and Barrett (*John*, p. 374) that this is nothing more than Passover piety. Both base their comments on Jeremias' works *The Eucharistic Words of Jesus* (1966, pp. 53f.) and *Jerusalem at the Time of Jesus* (1975, pp. 131ff.). However, Jeremias' reading is based on a reading back from sources such as *m.Pes.* 10.1, which orders that even the poor should receive four cups of wine on Passover eve, even if supported from the daily hand-out the *tamchuy* – *the pauper's dish*. However more recent work by Seccombe (1978 and 1982) comparing *m.Pes.* 10.1 and 5.1 show distinctions about what once happened in the temple and what should happen now. Seccombe questions just how public the charity was, its selectiveness, and questions any evidence for organised charity focused on the temple before AD 70 pointing out that there are no named temple officers with formal responsibility for the destitute *ptochoi*.

And again the destitute are not mentioned in the lists for emergency relief in difficult times. In the *Eucharistic Words* Jeremias cites the Mishnah, *Moed Pesachim* 9.11 and a 9th-century Aramaic prayer suggesting it was a regular practice to bring people off the street to share a meal. He suggests that Josephus report in *Ant.* 18.29f. that the gates of the temple were opened at midnight of Passover eve, implicitly allowed the beggars to congregate there. Although my reading of the Mishnah text is that it is about how to resolve a conflict involving a confusion over precedent in Passover offerings!

But the references to the common purse and to alms in John (6.5-7; 12.5-8; 13.29) seem to have nothing to do with Jeremias' late source prescriptive acts and anyway occur outside the context of the temple in Bethany (12.5-8) and Galilee (6.5-7).

In fact, if we go back to the driving of the money-changers from the temple at the first Johannine Passover (2.13-25) then there is of course a link between the money of the poor and the temple, but it implies an altogether different relationship. For Bauckham it is an attack on "the whole financial arrangements of the sacrifical system." (cited in Lindars, 1988). Then in 6.7 the second eve of Passover, the feeding of the 5,000 is a challenge to trust in food that satisfies rather than money (6.7,) but implicit in the account is the power of commonality, the sharing of what we have, leading to sufficiency and surplus, rather than the accumulation of personal and sectional wealth which never trickles down. And at the last Passover eve the disciples assume Judas is going to distribute to those destitute, again *ptochoi* (13.1-30), which Culpepper (*Anatomy of the Fourth Gospel*, 1983, p. 174) argues is a classic example of Johannine irony.

At the level of Johannine theology there is a clear line of development: the temple is a market place; money can't buy living bread; the real Passover gift to the destitute, the *ptochoi,* is not money but Jesus himself. Brown (*John I-XII*, pp. 543f.) interprets this as part of the author's christological intent, with Jesus now incarnating elements of Jewish covenantal practice, for example:

- 5.1-47 Jesus does what only God can do on the Sabbath
- 6.1-71 at Passover Jesus gives bread, replacing the manna of the Exodus
- 7-9 at Tabernacles Jesus symbolically becomes the water and light of the feast
- 5.2 at the sheep gate Jesus enters as the sheep to be freely sacrificed, and as the shepherd 10.1-21
- 10.22-39 at the Dedication Jesus is consecrated in place of the temple altar.

So is there a distinction between the practice of the Jesus group's almsgiving? If it is not simply a reflection of Passover practice, as Jeremias and those who follow him suggest, then is there anything else that can help us clarify it further?

Wider first-century cultural framework

It is not unique. Essene life, at least described by the first-century sources: Josephus, *BJ* (2)122; *Ant.* 18 (20); Philo *Hypothetica*, 10.4; *Quod omnis probus liber* 12.77; Pliny, *Natural History* 5.15.73; all speak of the pooling of resources among the celibate Essenes to provide a simple shared table and help to the destitute. Josephus *BJ* 2.8.6. (134) states: "Two things are left to individual discretion, the giving of assistance and mercy. Members may on their own decision help the deserving, when in need, and supply food to the destitute, but gifts to relatives are prohibited, without permission of the managers." B.J. Capper seems to be the scholar who has followed up this line as backcloth to his reflection on the economics of the New Covenant in an article in *IJSCC* 2 (2002), 9, 90.

The married Essene communities make monthly contribution to a common pot. The *Damascus Document* clarifies the role of those communities "and this is the rule of the many to provide for all their needs" (Capper, pp. 10-11). The *Damascus Document*, CD 14.12-17, speaks of a *beth-hacheber* community house which cared for "the needy and the poor, and the elder who is bowed down." Perhaps this gives a greater underpinning to Judas' protest at Mary's anointing of Jesus feet with pure nard at Bethany in 12.4-6: "Why was this ointment not sold for three hundred denarii and given to the poor (*ptochois*)?" The Benedictine archaeologist Bargil Pixner, from the Dormition Abbey in Jerusalem, has argued, along with others, for the location of an Essene house in Bethany (in R. Riesner, ed., *Wege des Messias und Stätten der Urkirche*, Basel, 1994, pp. 208-18). This would link with the reference in the *Temple Scroll* prescribing three villages to the east of Jerusalem dedicated to those ritually unclean and unable to enter the city (11QTTemple 46.16-17). Interestingly it is there that Mark 14.3 places Simon the Leper.

The etymology of the place indicates its function. Jerome translates it as *domus adflictionis* in his *Onomasticon*, which he derives from the Hebrew *beth 'anî*, or Aramaic *beth 'anyâ*, i.e. house of the poor, or of affliction, or poorhouse. So here we find Jesus and his disciples holding funds in common in a Judaean context where that practice is not unknown and is related to the giving of alms. Its perhaps also worth noting that, as far as I am aware, it is only at this place, Bethany, that the disciples show concern for the *ptochoi*. Perhaps out of shame, or embarrassment, given the well known practice of their neighbours.

The other reference to the common purse is the upper room in 13.29 but it is worth recording that it is also from the upper-room, *hyperoon*, in Acts 1.12-14 that the first community emerges at Pentecost, with from the start its characteristic emphasis on community of goods (Acts 2.42-47; 4.32–5.11; 6.1-6).

This custom of the disciple group is already commented on in Bultmann's 1971 commentary on the Bethany incident, where he states "It is then presupposed that the disciple group receives and distributes gifts for the poor, hence perhaps the custom reflected in Acts 4.37" (p. 415, n. 8).

Capper takes this further and suggests that the practice of the Essene communities having a gradually staged sharing of property depending on their commitment and stage of entrance in to the community can throw light on the whole Ananias incident in Acts 5.3-4 (cf. 1QS 6.18-20). If Ananias had followed the Essene practice of temporary donation, all would have been well.

Timothy Ling, whose 2006 monograph *The Judaean Poor and the Fourth Gospel* I have drawn on extensively, reflects on the development of the early Christian community in close proximity to the quarter in Jerusalem where archaeological work indicates the Essenes, or at least an ascetic group with similar practices, congregated (cf. the works of Pixner, Capper, Betz, and Riesner). Ling proposes that it is not insignificant that the two references in John to a common purse and the disciples' active concern for the *ptochoi* occur in Bethany, the house of the poor, and in the upper room which, if the work of Pixner and others is to be believed, was within the Essene quarter of Jerusalem.

One of the reasons the Essenes were so celebrated was their ideologically led practical commitment to ideals of justice and righteousness (*Thanksgiving Hymns*, 1QH 5.21-32) and their practical social organisation (cf. CD 14.12-17). Even to the point of designating themselves the "poor" (cf. 1QH 18.14; 1QM 11.9; 4QPs 37) with poverty here understood as total dependence on God (cf. 1QS 9.23-26). Ling (p. 179, n. 199), drawing on earlier work of Flusser, Miller, and J.A. Sanders, notes how the Essenes also draw on Isaiah 61, and the language of being anointed to bring glad tidings to the poor, as an expression of their embodying the fulfilment of God's word (cf. the use of Isa. 61.1-2 in 11QMelchizedek). Parallels are with Jesus' opening sermon in Luke 4.18.

Ling suggests that the Essenes understand this community to embody the new temple. The community's daily life now fulfilled the atoning sacrifices of the temple, effectively they are where the Temple truly is (cf. P.R. Davies, *Sects and Scrolls*, pp. 56f.).

It is John's Gospel above all that identifies Jesus' life with key elements of Hebrew religion and particularly the temple, in 2.19, 21 "Destroy this temple and in three days I will raise it up", and then again in 4.14 in the dialogue with the Samaritan woman, "the water I shall give will become a spring of water welling up to eternal life". The Spirit who is the source of true worship comes from Jesus, rather than the temple, replacing the need for cult and cult centre.

If we want a more truly indigenous contextual reading of Jesus' practice and engagement with the *ptochoi* and of the early communities commitment to a radical almsgiving and mutual use of property as expressed in 1 John 3.16f., with its radical identification of Jesus' self-offering and the brethren's quality of generosity, then we only have to look to the Essene's piety of poverty to give us an appropriate contextual and contemporaneous hermeneutic.

If my contextual reading has any merit it points to a capacity in the early Christian Community to go from the experience of radical empathy with the *ptochoi* into a re-reading of the Law and Prophets which then provides further stimulus for critical engagement with the religious structures, in their case the temple and the priesthood, which perpetuate such radical social division.

It also challenges us in following on this process in our own time to have the same freedom to use already existing religious and social means to further the gospel. The early followers of Jesus seemed able to utilise elements of the radical service of the poor witnessed to by some groups, possibly local Essene households, without being bound by their limiting reading of the ritual purity laws. Similarly there is no need for today's disciples to re-invent credit unions or food banks but every reason to participate in their development and use in the wider society.

Bibliography

Danby, H. (1933) *The Mishnah,* Oxford: Oxford University Press

Barrett, C.K. (1978) *The Gospel According to St. John,* Louisville: Westminster John Knox Press

Bauckham, R. (1988) "Jesus' demonstration in the Temple" in B. Lindars (ed.) *Law and Religion,* London: SPCK, pp. 72-89

Bultmann, R. (1971) *The Gospel of John,* Oxford: Blackwell

Brown, R.E. (1966) *The Gospel According to John,* 2 vols., London: Chapman

Capper, B.J. "The Church as the New Covenant of Effective Economics: The Social Origins of Mutually Supportive Christian Community", *IJSCC* 2 (2002), pp. 83-102

Culpepper, R.A. (1983) *Anatomy of the Fourth Gospel,* Philadelphia: Augsburg Fortress Press

Davies, P.R. (1996) *Sects and Scrolls: Essays in Qumran and Related Topics,* Atlanta: Scholars Press

Hamel, G. (1990 revised) *Poverty and Charity in Roman Palestine,* Berkeley, CA: University of California Press

Harland, P. (2002) "The Economy of First Century Palestine", in Blasi, Duha & Turcotte (eds.) *Handbook of Christianity: Social Science Approaches,* Walnut Creek, CA: Alta Mira Press, pp. 511-527

Ling, T. (2006) *The Judaean Poor and the Fourth Gospel,* SNTS Monograph 136, Cambridge: Cambridge University Press

Malina, B.J. & Rohrbaugh, R.L. (1998) *Social Science Commentary on the Gospel of John,* Philadelphia: Augsburg Fortress Press

Seccombe, D.P. (1978) "Was there organised charity in Jerusalem before the Christians?", *JTS* 29, 140-143

—— (1982) *Possessions and the Poor in Luke-Acts,* Linz: A. Fuchs.

7

Farewell Discourses as Retrospective Testimony

IAN WALLIS

It has long been my conviction that Holy Saturday delineates one of the most creative phases in the experience of Jesus' earliest followers. Although reduced to a 24-hour window within our Easter cycles, in real time its duration will have been much longer – characterised by grief, disorientation and crisis as well as a firm commitment to honour their master and continue his work – out of which emerged a profound awareness of Jesus' enduring presence: the concatenation of phenomena collectively described as resurrection.

I developed this thesis at length in *Holy Saturday Faith: Rediscovering the Legacy of Jesus.* If on the right lines, it invites a radically different reading of the Farewell Discourses within the Fourth Gospel. Namely, to interpret these chapters as one of the earliest experiments in what is now described as practice exegesis. Interpreted in this way, they originate in some of Jesus' bereft devotees who, after the crucifixion of their beloved teacher, drew on their memories of him and the fruits of their apprenticeship in his company, as they struggled to remain faithful to what Jesus had entrusted to them as well as to make sense of their predicament and embrace an uncertain, threatening future. What is more, as history testifies, they must have been exceptional practitioners, otherwise the Jesus movement would soon have died out and, with it, the impetus of faith and kingdom vision of its founder.

Thankfully, this did not happen and we are the beneficiaries of their legacy. In certain respects, we find ourselves in a comparable predicament to that of the disciples on the first Holy Saturday – with access only to a body of memories, now committed to writing, to realise Jesus' lively presence in our time and place. Given these similarities, it may prove insightful to reflect on the journey from memory to presence travelled by our pioneers in Practice Criticism to see what we can learn from their experiences in order to guide us in our performances.

The Fourth Gospel may seem an unlikely point of departure given that, compared with the Synoptics, its portrait of Jesus evidences considerable theological refashioning. However, as is increasingly recognised, embedded within its layers of mature reflection are hues and textures originating in earlier portrayals. Our focus of attention will be the *Farewell Discourses*, in which, within the context of the Last Supper (cf. John 13.4), Jesus prepares the disciples for his death and aftermath. The tenor is that of *anticipatory prediction* as Jesus stretches out the temporal canvas of the coming days, animating it with key happenings and experiences.

But the text can be viewed from another perspective, that of *retrospective testimony*. Here, the *Discourses* are structured and populated with recollections of what took place in real time. That is to say, the *Farewell Discourses* bear witness to the experiences of some of Jesus' earliest apprentices. What is more, by weaving these experiences within what amounts to Jesus' last will and testament, they are not only made visible for future apprentices but also elevated to canonical status through dominical authorisation. As such, they come to prescribe a process meriting emulation.

Read as retrospective testimony, the *Farewell Discourses* provide an object lesson in how the memory of Jesus was appropriated by his followers, leading to a fresh sense of his dynamic presence and fruitful ministry. What follows is an attempt to identify some of the key components in this process which are all seeded in the text awaiting retrieval. Here are the principal ones:

1. Prior to his death, the disciples were commissioned by Jesus to follow his example and to share his vocation.

> You call me Teacher and Lord – and you are right, for that is what I am. So if I, your Lord and Teacher, have washed your feet, you also ought to wash one another's feet. For I have set you an example, that you also should do as I have done to you [...] Very truly, I tell you, whoever receives one whom I send receives me; and whoever receives me receives him who sent me. (13.13–15, 20; NRSV here and throughout)

> You did not choose me but I chose you. And I appointed you to go and bear fruit, fruit that will last, so that the Father will give you whatever you ask him in my name. (15.16)

This is probably the least controversial component in that it represents an extrapolation of Jesus' call to discipleship and sacrificial service found in all the Gospels (e.g. Mark 1.16-20; 2.13-17; 8.34–9.1; 10.35-45; and parallels). Equally, I have argued elsewhere (*Illo Tempore*) that Jesus' actions at the last supper can plausibly be understood as a symbolic entrusting of his ministry into the hands of his apprentices and, at the same time, a commissioning of them to continue his vocation.

2. At the time of Jesus' arrest or crucifixion, the grouping of male disciples temporarily disintegrates.

> The hour is coming, indeed it has come, when you will be scattered, each one to his home, and you will leave me alone. (16.32)

The words to emphasize here are "male" and "temporarily." Mark, followed by Matthew, emphasizes the initial desertion of Jesus' gendered counterparts (Mark 14.27, 50/Matt 26.31, 56), while Luke and John attest their subsequent reformation (Luke 24.33; Acts 2.1; John 20.19, 26; 21.2). All four evangelists bear witness to the enduring companionship and faithfulness of the women disciples (Mark 15.40-41; 16.1-8; and parallels).

3. After Jesus' death, the disciples experience profound grief.

> Do not let your hearts be troubled. Believe in God, believe also in me. In my Father's house there are many dwelling-places. If it were not so, would I have told you that I go to prepare a place for you? And if I go and prepare a place for you, I will come again and will take you to myself, so that where I am, there you may be also [...] I will not leave you orphaned; I am coming to you. (14.1-3, 18)

> But because I have said these things to you, sorrow has filled your hearts [...] Very truly, I tell you, you will weep and mourn, but the world will rejoice; you will have pain, but your pain will turn into joy. When a woman is in labour, she has pain, because her hour has come. But when her child is born, she no longer remembers the anguish because of the joy of having brought a human being into the world. So you have pain now; but I will see you again, and your hearts will rejoice, and no one will take your joy from you. (16.6, 20-22; also 13.33, 36)

This should come as no surprise given the closeness and intensity of their relating, although the canonical Gospels only make grief explicit with reference to Jesus' female followers (Mark 16.1-8 and parallels). The *Gospel of Peter* surely states the obvious: "But I [i.e. Peter] mourned with my companions and, being wounded in heart, we hid ourselves for we were being sought after by them as if we were evil-doers and as persons who wanted to set fire to the temple. Besides all these things we were fasting and sat mourning and weeping night and day until the Sabbath." (7)

4. The disciples discover that by continuing in Jesus' pattern of love and service they remain close to him and, as a consequence, are able to share his experience of God.

> Very truly, I tell you, the one who believes in me will also do the works that I do and, in fact, will do greater works than these, because I am going to the Father. I will do whatever you ask in my name, so that the Father may be glorified in the Son. If in my name you ask me for anything, I will do it. If you love me, you will keep my commandments [...] They who have my commandments and keep them are those who love me; and those who love me will be loved by my Father, and I will love them and reveal myself to them [...] Those who love me will keep my word, and my Father will love them, and we will come to them and make our home with them. Whoever does not love me does not keep my words; and the word that you hear is not mine, but is from the Father who sent me [...] Peace I leave with you; my peace I give to you. I do not give to you as the world gives. Do not let your hearts be troubled, and do not let them be afraid. (14.12–15, 21, 23–24, 27)

> Abide in me as I abide in you. Just as the branch cannot bear fruit by itself unless it abides in the vine, neither can you unless you abide in me. I am the vine, you are the branches. Those who abide in me and I in them bear much fruit, because apart from me you can do nothing. Whoever does not abide in me is thrown away like a branch and withers; such branches are gathered, thrown into the fire, and burned. If you abide in me, and my words abide in you, ask for whatever you wish, and it will be done for you. My Father is glorified by this, that you bear much fruit and become my disciples. As the Father has loved me, so I have loved you; abide in my love. If you keep my commandments, you will abide in my love, just as I have kept my Father's commandments and abide in his love. (15.4–10; also 13.34–35; 14.6–14; 16.26–27)

Josephus, the first-century Jewish historiographer with Roman sympathies, was no supporter of the Jesus movement. For this reason his minimal reference to it is all the more revealing:

> At this time there appeared Jesus, a wise man [if indeed one should call him a man]. For he was a doer of startling deeds, a teacher of people who receive the truth with pleasure. And he gained a following both among many Jews and among many of Greek origin. [He was the Messiah.] And when Pilate, because of an accusation made by the leading men among us, condemned him to the cross, those who had loved him previously did not cease to do so. [For he appeared to them on the third day, living again, just as the divine prophets had spoken of these and countless other wondrous things about him.] And up until this very day the tribe of Christians, named after him, has not died out. (*Antiquities* 18.3.3 §63–64)

The sections in square brackets are generally considered to be later Christian interpolations. What is significant for us is where Josephus locates the impetus for the continuation of the Jesus movement – "those who had loved him previously did not cease to do so."

5. The disciples intuit a "spiritual persona" or "alter-ego", mediating Jesus' presence by acting as a source of guidance, inspiration and remembrance, discrete from themselves and capable of maintaining his accessibility.

> And I will ask the Father, and he will give you another Advocate, to be with you for ever. This is the Spirit of truth, whom the world cannot receive, because it neither sees him nor knows him. You know him, because he abides with you, and he will be in you. I will not leave you orphaned; I am coming to you. In a little while the world will no longer see me, but you will see me; because I live, you also will live. On that day you will know that I am in my Father, and you in me, and I in you [...] But the Advocate, the Holy Spirit, whom the Father will send in my name, will teach you everything, and remind you of all that I have said to you. (14.16–20, 26)

> Nevertheless I tell you the truth: it is to your advantage that I go away, for if I do not go away, the Advocate will not come to you; but if I go, I will send him to you [...] I still have many things to say to you, but you cannot bear them now. When the Spirit of truth comes, he will guide you into all the truth; for he will not speak on his own, but will speak whatever he hears, and he will declare to you the things that are to come. He will glorify me, because he will take what is mine and declare it to you. All that the Father has is mine. For this reason I said that he will take what is mine and declare it to you. (16.7, 12–15; also 15.26–27)

Whilst passages such as these lay out in some detail the ways in which Jesus was experienced spiritually as a dynamic presence after the crucifixion, this phenomenon is repeatedly attested in early Christian literature (e.g. Acts 16.7; Romans 8.9; Philippians 1.19; 1 Peter 1.11; Revelation 19.10), mediating resurrection. Evidently, Paul's call or conversion was effected by a profound spiritual experience of the risen Christ (Galatians 1.15-16; 1 Corinthians 15.3-8).

6. The disciples encounter opposition and persecution for continuing to follow Jesus, which has the effect of confirming their conviction that he is still with them and authenticating their commitment to following in his way.

> If the world hates you, be aware that it hated me before it hated you. If you belonged to the world, the world would love you as its own. Because you do not belong to the world, but I have chosen you out of the world – therefore the world hates you. Remember the word that I said to you, "Servants are not greater than their master." If they persecuted me, they will

persecute you; if they kept my word, they will keep yours also. But they will do all these things to you on account of my name, because they do not know him who sent me. (15.18–21)

I have said these things to you to keep you from stumbling. They will put you out of the synagogues. Indeed, an hour is coming when those who kill you will think that by doing so they are offering worship to God. And they will do this because they have not known the Father or me [...] I have said this to you, so that in me you may have peace. In the world you face persecution. But take courage; I have conquered the world! (16.1–3, 33)

Again, persecution of the Jesus movement in its nascent years was a regular occurrence, precipitated by a range of motivations (e.g. Mark 13.9-13; Acts 8.1; 16.16-40; 19.23-41; Romans 12.14; 1 Thessalonians 3.1-8; Hebrews 10.32-33; Revelation 2.8-11).

By approaching the *Farewell Discourses* as retrospective testimony originating in the experiences of some of the disciples around the time of Jesus' death rather than as anticipatory prediction made by Jesus on the occasion of the Last Supper to prepare them for what to expect, we gain access to an alternative account of how Jesus came to life in the experience of his followers, post mortem. What is more, given the uniqueness of chapters 13–17, it is conceivable that they give expression to resurrection within the experience not only of some of Jesus' first followers but also members of the Johannine community who, temporally divorced from the appearance traditions referred to by Paul in 1 Corinthians 15.3-8 and given narrative form in three of the four Gospel accounts, were able to move beyond second-hand testimony to relate to Jesus as a living memory and dynamic presence for themselves.

Five phases within this early attempt of practice criticism can be identified, the first being the disciples' appropriation of a particular memory of Jesus' words and actions, the execution of his last will and testament, which were most probably performed during the final meal they shared together before his arrest, trial and crucifixion:

Commission - Entrusting of Jesus' "kingdom" vision and vocation

Absence – Jesus dies and is no longer physically present

Faithfulness – the disciples embrace Jesus' vision and vocation

Presence – Jesus "spiritually" inhabits their faithfulness

Opposition – the disciples, like their master, face persecution

What is striking about this progression is the relationship between practice and presence. According to the appearance traditions, encountering the resurrected Jesus transformed the disciples' grief into joy, their despondency into faith, their inertia into service – *presence precipitated practice*. By contrast, the *Farewell Discourses* bear witness to a different ordering, namely that it was the commitment of the disciples to embrace what Jesus had entrusted to them in terms of continuing his ministry which provided the context for encounter, for participating in the living memory of Jesus – *practice engendered presence*.

This insight carries far-reaching implications for contemporary discipleship, placing the emphasis firmly upon practice – participation in Jesus' kingdom vision through embodied faith – as the process mediating resurrection. Jesus comes to life in the experience of those who remember him through fresh performances of his ministry and imaginative improvisations of his way.

One sphere where this will have a significant impact is Christian nurture and faith-development. The "practice engenders presence" paradigm favours an apprenticeship model where the emphasis falls upon becoming proficient practitioners in the artistry of faith, rather than upon embracing a system of belief or participating in particular kinds of religious experience. From this perspective, Jesus becomes the paradigmatic artisan whose embodiment of faith informs Christian discipleship and inspires emulation. Central to this approach is identifying the foundational insights and components of faith's artistry before developing induction programmes for their dissemination. For example, amongst those elements would be practising forgiveness, cultivating wisdom, living hospitably, learning to love, pursuing justice and fostering mindfulness. Churches then take on the function of becoming communities where these are celebrated and inculcated through iteration, emulation and experimentation within a relatively safe environment with a view to encouraging practice throughout life.

To work effectively, this approach needs to become embedded in all aspects of church life, including worship where it finds ritual expression. For many denominations this will require new liturgical resources in addition to those already authorized for use. The following Thanksgiving (Eucharistic) Prayer, based on Isaiah 58, illustrates how these emphases can be incorporated into traditional forms:

God of the Jubilee,
in Christ, you shatter the temples
we create to contain you
and reveal your will
to loose the bonds of injustice
and let the oppressed go free,
to share your bread with the hungry
and shelter the homeless poor.

Silence our pretensions
and prepare our hearts
to suffer the cries of your suffering people
and respond with the offering of our lives.

With all in every age
who have been stirred by your passion
or longed for your presence,
who yearn for your light to break forth like the dawn
and your healing to spring up swiftly,
we raise our voices in acclamation.

Holy, holy, holy Lord,
God of truth and love,
heaven and earth are full of your glory.
Hosanna in the highest.

Blessed is he who comes in the name of the Lord.
Hosanna in the highest.

Especially, we praise you
for coming among us in Jesus,
in him, your kingdom is made manifest,
through him, your will is fulfilled,
with him, we are called into service.

And now,
in obedience to his command,
it is our duty and our joy,
to remember the night he gave himself up
and was handed over to death.

One final time,
in the company of his own,
gathered around a table,
Jesus took bread, gave thanks,
broke it and offered it to them,
saying, "This is my life,"
all that I embody,
I entrust it to you.

Later, he took a cup of wine,
gave thanks and offered it to them, saying,
"With this we celebrate our new relationship with God,"
forged from forgiveness,
sealed with my blood.
This is how you will remember me.

It will also be necessary to develop whole-church learning programmes. *The Art of Living* is one such course which seeks to create a playful ambience in which participants relax and enjoy the experience of learning together through experimentation. In keeping with this approach, Jesus takes on the guise of the fool, nicknamed Wilf (an acronym), who acts as guide for those intrigued by the question, What is life for? Faith is presented as a journey of discovery with various insights and life-skills introduced *en route*:

Fool's Paradise – The art of living life as a gift

Playing the Fool – The art of praying

Fool's Gold – The art of wisdom

Fool's Errand – The art of loving

Feast of Fools – The art of hospitality

The emphasis throughout is upon inquiry-led, person-centred learning within a communal setting – a permissory space in which everyone is encouraged to participate playfully. Each insight or life-skill is introduced by a Gospel story about Jesus followed by exploration of how he practised it within the context of his ministry. So, for instance, considerable time is devoted to identifying instances of Jesus, say, living gratuitously, cultivating openness and compassion, applying wisdom, embodying love, being hospitable.

Reflection on Jesus' improvisation of the art of living encourages participants to start thinking about how these core insights and life-skills inform the life of the church community and have the potential to animate their lives also. With respect to the latter, the aim is to build upon what is already in place as well as to stress their application through the whole of life and not just restricted to so-called religious dimensions. Here, mentoring can be helpful with the more experienced supporting those just starting off. Each member is supplied with a "Passport to Life" (a log of personal engagement with the programme) which accompanies them throughout and provides a permanent record of the journey undertaken and the outcomes realised. The course is intentionally light on theology, placing emphasis upon practice and experience, presenting Jesus as teacher, practitioner and guide who embodies his gospel and enables others to do likewise – faith's pioneer and fulfiller (cf. Hebrews 12.2).

Bibliography

Ashton, J. *Understanding the Fourth Gospel* (Oxford: Clarendon, 1991).

——— (ed.), *The Interpretation of John* (2nd ed., Edinburgh: T. & T. Clark, 1997)

Brown, R.E. *The Gospel According to John: A New Translation with Introduction and Commentary*, 2 vols. (2nd ed., New York: Doubleday, 1981)

Burge, G.M. *The Anointed Community: The Holy Spirit in the Johannine Tradition* (Grand Rapids, MI: Eerdmans, 1987)

Dodd, C.H. *The Interpretation of the Fourth Gospel* (Cambridge: Cambridge University Press, 1953)

———, *Historical Tradition in the Fourth Gospel* (Cambridge: Cambridge University Press, 1963)

Käsemann, E. *The Testament of Jesus* (trans. G. Krodel; London: SCM, 1968)

Köstenberger, A.J. *The Missions of Jesus and the Disciples according to the Fourth Gospel with Implications for the Fourth Gospel's Purpose and the Mission of the Contemporary Church* (Grand Rapids, MI: Eerdmans, 1998)

Martyn, J.L. *History and Theology in the Fourth Gospel* (2nd ed., Nashville: Abingdon, 1979)

Smith, D.M. *Johannine Christianity: Essays on its Setting, Sources, and Theology* (Columbia, SC: University of South Carolina, 1984)

Thatcher, T. *Why John Wrote a Gospel: Jesus, Memory, History* (Louisville, KY: Westminster John Knox, 2006)

Wallis, I. *Holy Saturday Faith: Rediscovering the Legacy of Jesus* (London: SPCK, 2000)

———, "The Last Supper as Jesus' Last Will and Testament", in *Illo Tempore* 25 (2004), pp. 3-17.

8

Divinity in Disciples

JOHN VINCENT

1. Jesus and Disciples in John

The Johannine way begins with the practice of the disciple. Their love
for each other is the sign by which they are recognised (13.35). By
"keeping the word of God", disciples secure the manifestation of the
Father and Jesus. Disciples choose the will of God (7.17), as Jesus himself
does (4.34).

The Johannine disciple has to follow Jesus. The classic synoptic term
for following (*akolouthein*) is used in 1.43. The disciples continue the
"discipleship" role that Jesus performs in relation to his Father. Jesus is
the light of the world (8.12; 9.5), and disciples are "children of light"
(12.36). Jesus shows what he has seen of his Father's practice (5.20-36).
Disciples "testify" (4.29, 4.39, 6.14) what they behold of Jesus' practice
as son.

But this testimony to Jesus by disciples is, like Jesus' testimony to his
Father, much more in action than in word. Their loving activity towards
each other (13.35; 15.15-17) is repeating Jesus' love for them. (13.1, 34).
Each continues divine activities performed by Jesus, as does their washing of each other's feet (13.15), continuing Jesus' washing of their feet
(13.1-8). Likewise, their future martyrdom continues his martyrdom
(15.18; 3.16), which is the result of the Father's love for his Son (3.16).
The "New Commandment" of love is that someone lays down their life
for their friends (15.13), in imitation of what Jesus does for his friends
(10.14). In 17.10, "all that is the Father's is mine", and by Jesus' prayer
for "those whom you have given me" (17.9) is also now the possession
of the disciples. "Through them has my glory shone" (17.10), and they
share the Father's glory (17.22). They remain in the world, in the same
way as Jesus was in the world (17.11). They now possess the word
(17.14). As the Father sent Jesus into the world, so Jesus sends the disciples (17.18). For their sake has Jesus consecrated himself (17.19).

Here the mission of the apostles is taken up into the supreme moment of the mission of the Son in which the task appointed him by the Father is completed.[1]

The image of Jesus as the vine achieves its climax in the fruit that it brings forth (15.5) – fruit that has abiding value (15.4), fruit that is plentiful, which ensures that the disciples are true disciples (15.8). Such fruit is a guarantee that Christ is present in the disciple (15.3). The vine itself indicates that Jesus and his disciples are equally parts of the same reality (15.5-6).

In 9.3, 14.12 and 15.24 the disciples imitate Jesus in performing miracles, though their actions only precipitate the world's hatred, as his have done (15.18). In 15.20 the disciples explicitly do what the master does. "The slave is not greater than his Lord." The true slave will be treated as the Lord is treated. On the issue that Jesus has just called them "friends", Wes Howard-Brook comments:

> The disciples are both Jesus' equals as friends who do his works and greater ones and his slaves who have life only if they remain in union with him. At least they are equal in being mistreated and ignored by the world![2]

Outsiders do not keep Jesus' word and will not keep the disciples' word either (15.20).

> No-one has ever seen the Father, but the only Son has made him known (1.18). Disciples have seen this "glory" (1.14), and make him known (21.24).

Jesus and disciples both speak (17.22) and do works (17.24). "Word and works are opposite sides of the single coin in Jesus' mission as well as that of his followers."[3]

2. The Works

The words of John concerning "the works" are highly significant:

The Father in me	
is doing the works that I do	(14-10b)
If you cannot believe the Father is in me	
then believe me because of the works that I do	(14.11)
The believer in me	
will do the works that I do	
And because I am going back to the Father	
will do greater works than these	(14.12)

---

[1] C.K. Barrett, *The Gospel According to St John*, London: SPCK, 1955, p. 421.

[2] Wes Howard-Brook, *Becoming Children of God: John's Gospel and Radical Discipleship*, Maryknoll, NY: Orbis Books, 1994, p. 339.

[3] Wes Howard Brook, *Becoming Children of God*, p. 340.

It is already in John 10:

> If I'm not doing the Father's work,
> then don't believe me. (10.37)
> But if I'm doing the Father's work,
> then even if you don't believe me,
> Believe the works! (10.38)

What are the greater works promised in 14.12? Wes Howard-Brook romanticises:

> The result of faith – if they can muster it – is to do works "greater" than those of Jesus! What possible greater works are left to do? Jesus has healed the sick, given sight to the blind, and raised the dead. He has overturned the temple tables, replaced the entire spectrum of Judean rituals, and spoken truth to power. He has broken open the bounds of "God's People" to include Samaritans and Greeks. The one work he has not done yet is *to establish a continuing community of faith to follow in his footsteps* when he has departed. At Jesus' death, there will be few left, and even after his resurrection, the disciples remain scattered and scared. It will be *their* job to reap the harvest (4.38). By the time of the gospel, of course, this "greater" work was already partly in the past, although the long-term existence of the Johannine community and the wider Christian family remained in great doubt. This is indeed a greater work than any individual healing or short-term institutional challenge, for it is the necessary step in assuring that Jesus' life and teaching will be remembered.[4]

"A continuing Community of Faith to follow in his footsteps" does not sound exactly the same as Jesus doing the works in his Father's footsteps! Surely, we must speak of "a continuing Community of Works to do the works that he does". Following without performance is unthinkable. But it is the works, not the following, that are the continuing divine reality in John's schema. And John's concern is not that "Jesus' life and teaching will be remembered", but that Jesus' practice imitative of the divine practice shall continue to be practised, in this case by his disciples.

Precisely this repetition and carrying on of the Master's actions and works is required by disciples as servants. As servants, the basic thing is that they carry out meticulously what the Master wishes, which is what the disciples as servants have done, even when they did not know "what his Master is about" (15.15).

One reaction to this has been a growth in "political" interpretations of John. Thus, David Rensberger argues for a "Johannine sectarianism" that combats the dangers of closedness and introversion by confronting

---

[4] Wes Howard Brook, *Becoming Children of God*, p. 317.

the world with "an alternative society", a counter-culture, in which its message of the messiahship of Jesus was realised.

> In this standing against the world it puts its own life in the world at risk, for it must always recall the words of Jesus before his Passion: "If anyone serves me, let that person follow me, and where I am there will my servant be also" (12.26).[5]

Certainly, following and servanthood are the decisive elements, rather than contemplation and mystical union.

3. Divine Recapitulation in Disciples

The Johannine scheme sees the disciple as the decisive "delivery point" of revelation. Jesus promises "when I am not here, I will send the Paraclete to you" (11.7), and the paraclete will assist the realities and practice of divine life on earth. The "all things" placed in Jesus' hands by his Father (3.35) are now handed over by the Son to the Disciples (15.15).

The Father has given me	
all that I have	(16.15)
The Spirit will hand on to you what he hears/sees	
from what is mine	(16.14)
The Spirit, who issues from the Father,	
will bear witness to me.	(15.26)
And you also bear witness to me	
because you have been with me from the start.	(15.27)

As C.K. Barrett says on v. 27, "The Spirit and the disciples both continue the work of Jesus", and "the disciples' unity with him (as the last discourses constantly repeat) can never be permanently broken".[6]

In a term of seminars on John's Gospel, Henry J. Cadbury commented on "I will send you a Paraclete from the Father": "But doesn't God send the Paraclete (14.16, 26)?", then jokingly, "But then, it doesn't matter: It's all between friends."[7]

There certainly is a "friendship" between Father and Son, which Jesus then extends to his disciples as his "friends", "because I have passed on to you everything I heard from my Father" (15.15).

The sequence and the unity may be best stated on the model of 5.16–22.

---

[5] David Rensberger, *Overcoming the World: Politics and Community in the Gospel of John*, London: SPCK, 1988, p. 150.

[6] C.K. Barrett, *John*, pp. 402-403.

[7] Prof. Henry J. Cadbury at Drew Theological Seminary, Madison, NJ, 1954-55.

The Father continually works, now the Son also works (5.17). The Son can do nothing by himself. He does only what he sees the Father doing. Whatever the Father does, the Son does (5.19).

For the Father loves the Son and shows him all his actions. And he will show greater yet, so that you will be astonished (5.20).

The "greater yet" probably refers to consequent disciple action, like the "greater things" of 14.12. The activity and consciousness, the works and the words, of the disciple continue those of Jesus, which continue those of God.

> If anyone loves me, he will hold to my word,
>   and my Father will love him.
> We will come to him
>   and make our dwelling in/with him (4.13)

In 17.22, Jesus is reported as saying

> The glory which you gave to me I have given to them so that they may be in union with us, just as we are in union with each other.

The "being in union" in this whole context must mean "being in union with Father and Son", not simply "being in union with each other"

Jesus and disciple have almost identical roles and functions. Jesus is "The Way, the Truth and the Life" (14.6). Disciples do not need to know where they are going. Indeed, the destination is kept secret in 13.33–14.3. But the point is that "you know the way – you don't need to know the destination" (14.4). Jesus' destination is "my Father" (14.12).

Jesus claims his disciples as part of the divine revelation which he himself is. The way that they are treated is a sign of their being his disciples. Their being persecuted is a sign of this (17.14). Hence the warning of 16.2. Persecution is a form of communion with Christ (15.20-21, 23), by which God's judgment on the cosmos is revealed (15.24).[8]

Is there a pre-existing commonality of humans with divinity?

Jesus' response to the accusation that "you, a mere human, are claiming to be God (or 'a god')" in 10.33, 34:

> It is not written in your law, "I said: you are gods". They to whom the word of God was delivered are called gods – and scripture cannot be set aside.

Jesus, "asking as my Father would", uses a text to justify his actions which at least opens the door to a claim that humans, made gods, would naturally do what the Father of a Son would show to his Son (10.36),

---

[8] Cf. C.H. Dodd, *The Interpretation of the Foruth Evangelist*, Cambridge: Cambridge University Press, 1984, pp. 412-413.

due to a mutual indwelling of Father and Son (10.38) – in this case the Son being not a special individual, but the human race, all human beings.

4. Disciples as Revelation

The Johannine schema envisages a continuing reality of revelation, not only as the early disciples carry on their work, but also in those who become disciples through them. Jesus thus prays:

> I ask not only on behalf of these, but also on behalf of those who will believe in me through their word, that they may all be in a single reality ("one") (17.20).

Specifically, this will extend the divine reality on earth.

> As you, Father, are in me, and I am in you, they may also be in (both of) us. (17.21)

The result is that the world, seeing them, may also see the Son and the Father behind them (17.21).

It has been suggested by Paul S. Minear that later disciples are intended, that this wider grouping indicates a second generation of disciples, and that "a generation gap is recognised in the very effort to overcome it". Both generations are part of the same reality possessing the same *name,* the same *glory*, the same *love*: Daniel Stevick comments:[9]

> The church is united in the *name* that came from God and that thus sustains the community (vv. 11b, 12); it held a common *glory* given now (v. 22) and pledged for the future (v. 24); and it is bound by the *love* which came from God and was bestowed first on the son and through him on the church, where it was lodged in each believer (vv. 23, 26b).[10]

In the Johannine scheme, disciples – then and presumably now – are the fourth – or the billionth, billion and fourth – living persons of the Trinity! John's Gospel invites you to work in a continuing mystery, the divine incarnation in Christ continuing in you. You are now the Vessel, the "pot of clay" in which the divine life originating in eternity in the Father, manifest in time in the Son, perpetuated in history in the Spirit, now has a continuing life on earth. A Divinisation is taking place as the image of the Son takes over within you – "Christ in you" – the reality of God. The prayer, "that they all might be united in One" (17.21) obviously refers simply to the common dynamic and practice of living and caring, flowing through each of the members and groups.

---

[9] Paul S. Minear, "The Audience of the Fourth Evangelist", *Interpretation* 31, 1977, 340-346, 344.
[10] Daniel B. Stevick, *Jesus and His Own, A Commentary on John 13–17*, Grand Rapids/Cambridge: Eerdmans, 2011, p. 359.

But how does this take place? Not primarily by nature but primarily by practice. The model for the disciple is Jesus doing the things of the Father. So, now, the disciple does – the things of the Son, Jesus. The "Word" has been made "Flesh", the "Nature" has become "Reality", first in Jesus and then in disciples.

John's Gospel puts it in a human model – a model of four Gods standing behind each other:

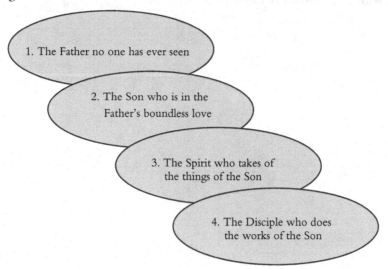

1. The Father no one has ever seen

2. The Son who is in the Father's boundless love

3. The Spirit who takes of the things of the Son

4. The Disciple who does the works of the Son

The decisive, determinative, distinctive one of the four is the second, the one who practices the practice that makes possible its visibility in all that follows.

5. Practice Today

A flood of experiences now find their theology.

I confine myself to my own tiny bailiwick – two pieces of experience in the life of the Ashram Community in Sheffield, just this last year.

We have fortnightly Gathering in each other's homes, with bring-and-share meals, followed by community prayers and concerns and then a topic, introduced by members in turn. The series in 2014 was "Favourite Texts". Ruth Bird, a retired nursing sister, introduced her own experiences of healing by touch, of communion through breaking bread, of giving others the sacrament, of serving and joining in the "Burngreave Banquet" Wednesday evening free meal. It was, she said, a continuation of Theresa of Avila: "He has no hands but your hands now."

Ten days later, we had half a dozen visitors with us for a three-day inner-city retreat. Its inspiration and organiser, Nirmal Fernando, describes its purpose thus:

Be a 'guest' welcomed as Jesus
In a community home
Sharing around the table as he did,
Contemplating on his Gospel and life
Expressing insights with one another
En-fleshing his words in our beings,
Walking the city streets as he did
With a Community of caring Disciples!

9

Jesus' Recall to Discipleship in John 21

NIRMAL FERNANDO

1. Discipleship and Community

> The early disciples ... did not put work as their first priority. Even a source of income did not come first. The kingdom ... came first, and usually led to the disciple leaving ... work ... (Vincent 1984: 39).

To me, this becomes apparent in a penetrative and reflective reading of the "Gospels". It portrays the disciples living in microcommunity with Jesus as their leader and teacher, transforming their own private homes and those facilitated by others into community spaces and dwellings – a sharing of each other's resources caringly.[1] Their way of life is not dependent on corporate grants from state or charities, wage labour, salaries, trade (fair or unfair) or profits from business. Denying self, risking self-security and seeking no assurances whatsoever, they become self-resourcing by transforming what is private to be communal without quantitative measure. This, and voluntary donations from some benefactors, which were perhaps magnanimous, ensured that there was no one lacking among them. This radical alternative way of life was probably relieved of the burdens of conventional social-economy with its perpetual sectors of exploiters and exploited, haves and have-nots. In effect, Jesus and his disciples clearly transcended the dual categories of private and public in implementing the communal.

It is also apparent that all these socioeconomic features which made that independent intentional community viable were centrally hinged on the individual Jesus. Throughout every page of the "Gospels" it is not a following of or devotedness to the disciples or any other, but a following of or devotedness to Jesus. It is Jesus the central personage that brings all things to commonality, and certainly that attracts significant donations and support. This model continues in Christian Intentional Communities today (Vincent, ed., 2011: Davies & Fernando, 2014).

---

[1] See Luke 8.1-3, "... ministered unto him of their substance" (Gk: *hyparchonta*; possessions, goods, wealth, property).

Therefore, it is highly probable that this infrastructure was in disarray, and whatever support was stalled if not intentionally withdrawn, after the terrifying death of Jesus. This is quite understandable given the entailing fear, doubts and serious reservations among disciples, followers and benefactors alike as to the viable continuity of the mission which had barely lasted three years.

Further, the community's trusted "treasurer",[2] having breached his trust was no longer around. It is most probable that all the liquid assets of the community had disappeared with his demise.[3]

On the other hand, the connectedness of the disciples appears not to have been fully fragmented after the death of Jesus, as is apparent in the narratives. In fact, the freedom of non-privacy among them is seen by the benign "nakedness" of a disciple, Peter, recorded at John 21.7, our focus chapter in this paper.

2. Preparedness for Separation

John 21 commences by describing a group of Jesus' disciples, including the leading players in the narrative (21.2), returning to their former work and possibly the conventional way of life that they had renounced some years ago. This was probably because of disillusion and perhaps in order to survive, due to the lack of community resources which had no doubt provided them with needed basics for two to three years. The firm decision of Peter, perhaps an experienced fisherman, the immediate following of the others without any dithering, and the urgency with which they put to sea that evening is clear (21.3). This was no leisurely excursion; they fished all night up until dawn, obviously hoping for a good catch, but nothing was netted! Then, the resurrected Jesus standing on the shore, perhaps sensing their lack of resources, enquires of their catch and advises rightly. The unquestioning disciples do as they are told, resulting in a highly exceptional large catch! (21.4-6). John Wesley commenting on v. 6 states "… a kind supply for them … when they waited afterward in Jerusalem" (Wesley 1754: 388). We now know that there was in place an established and lucrative salt fish industry on the shores of the Sea of Galilee supplying not only the Palestinian market but also exports to the West including Rome (Bouquet 1953: 73-74). The exact counting of the number of fish (21.11) also suggests probably a wholesale industry.

---

[2] John 12.4-6.
[3] Matt 27.3-10.

The only recorded instance of Jesus addressing his disciples collectively, using the Greek word *paidion* (metaphorically: children; like children in intellect) occurs in our text at 21.5.[4] He, having called them to leave or even abandon all else, follow him, implicitly accept him as leader and teacher unreservedly, is no longer there with them as was usual, because of the decision he took to leave them, intentionally and by choice.[5] Jesus understands that they depended exclusively on his centrality for physical, psychological and emotional needs. Despite some three years of intense radical alternative community experience with him, they are now returning to the conventional way of life. Most importantly, their mind-set is like a band of abandoned children without a parent to turn to.

Hence Peter's joyous leap into the waters after hearing of Jesus' presence on the shore. He rushes and swims to his master who was unexpected, having little patience to wait until the vessel now pulling an unusually heavy cargo reaches land (21.7-8). It is perhaps a loss that we have no record of the dialogue and/or occurrences that took place between Jesus and Peter before the other disciples joined them on shore. Similarly, we have no details of Jesus' post-resurrection appearance exclusively to Peter mentioned at Luke 24.34 and 1 Cor. 15. 5. Now, Jesus obviously had a special place for Peter, being one of the three that he called apart several times according to the narratives. Apart from that, it appears that Jesus had a special confidence in Peter, evidenced at Matt. 16.18-19. Further, Jesus was fully aware of Peter's deep reverence, loyalty and surrender of self-will, narrated in the text describing Jesus' washing of the feet of his disciples (John 13.6-9). Jesus rightly understood his relative dependability, particularly in crisis, since it was Peter alone that tried to resist the arrest of Jesus (John 18.10); followed him to his place of trial (Mark 14.54; John 18.15; Matt. 26.58; Luke 22.54-55), and fearlessly entered before John into the empty tomb (John 20.6).

3. Continuing Community

Jesus commences by asking them to share of their catch (21.10) with the food that he had (21.9) and eat in community (21.12). As usual Jesus breaks the bread (and fish likewise) and gives it to the disciples (21.13), symbolising the unreserved selfless giving in community, even unto death and after it. This is the only post-resurrection record of the Lord calling disciples to his table, which obviously was a potent reminder to

---

[4] Jesus uses another Greek word, *teknion*, addressing the disciples after Judas's departure at the last supper, as at John 13.33 – literally meaning a little child, but in the NT used as a term of kindly address by teachers to their disciples.

[5] See John 16.7; and that passage read together with John 14.16, 26, and 15.26.

them not only of the Last Supper, but also of many previous meals where Jesus and the community would have done likewise, sharing food, the basic necessity of community life.

4. Leadership Provisions

After meeting that basic need, not addressing all the disciples at the "table", yet with them decisively gathered together at a vital community meeting, Jesus specifically addresses Peter. The brief questioning dialogue reveals the firm intention of Jesus unilaterally (with absolutely no consultation whatsoever with the community) to assign Peter a vital task-role within the community, subject to Peter's unreserved commitment even though it will ultimately bring about his execution (21.18-19). Although Jesus' questioning and assigning appears to be repetitive, on reflection it is clear that subtle and vital intentional differences were there in the mind of Jesus along with a possible reason for apparent repetition.

"… More than *these?*" (21.15) in the first question probably refers to "these things" or "these matters" (Gk: *toutōn*). I would suggest that Jesus meant matters of the kingdom of mammon, such as conventional socio-economic life. It certainly did not mean the others in community, for there is no record of any reaction from the disciples.

5. Parting Words of Love

Turning to the word love, it is interesting and important that Jesus uses the Gk *agapaō, selfless and unconditional love,* in the first two questions, but Peter replies using *phileō, to treat affectionately or kindly, to welcome, befriend, to approve of, sanction* (21.15, 16). Given Peter's usage of the term implying love and loyalty with interest of the personage of Jesus, Jesus uses Peter's term *phileō* in the third question and Peter replies in the same (21.17). However, what Peter is asked to undertake in action, provided he has selfless and unconditional love or even loyal love to Jesus, is to "feed" Jesus' "flock", which is primarily the communities of disciples (21.15-17). Two terms translated as "feed" are used by Jesus in Greek: *boskō, spiritual (psycho-emotional) needs,* and *poimainō, nourish physically, serve the body,* also *to supply the requisites for "spiritual" needs.*

Apart from Luke's usage in the parable (Luke 15.6) it is only the Johannine narrative that uses the phrase "my sheep" on the lips of Jesus. It is found at John 10.14, 26, 27; and verses 16 and 17 in our text. In all these instances not only are they words of Jesus, but appear to be used in reference to those who hear his teaching and follow his way of life (10.27), specifically excluding those who do not (John 10.26, 14). In fact, the Greek term attributed here to Jesus is *mou, of me.* Hence, Jesus' assignment to Peter, is to take over the leadership/facilitation[6] in a central praxis of setting in place physical, psychological and emotional caring and sharing within the discipleship community (allegorised – sheep live in a flock), since Jesus was unable to do that any more. A priority appears to have been given to those who need most, signified by "lambs" (21.15) in the first assignment mentioned in the text, for we know that among them there were those yet lacking in confidence even at the ascension (Matt 28.16-17).

To my mind, Jesus hurt and annoyed Peter (21.17) by repeated questioning with loving intent in the interests of the discipleship community. With Peter in that state, Jesus mentions his future execution resulting from the return to the radical alternative way of life and his role of leadership therein. This was a foretaste of the extreme tolerance vital in the mission assigned to Peter. Then Jesus tells an unruffled Peter, "Follow me" (21.18-19): also an example to the eyes of the others in community.

The dialogue relating to the disciple whom Jesus loved, who also followed them (21.20-23), perhaps taught Peter and all intentional disciples never to compare one's role in discipleship with that of others in the community. For there is no room for measure of vocation, sacrifice, or reward in the Kingdom of God on earth.

It is nothing but ideal that this is the ending narrative in the Johannine biography of Jesus – the recall to and handing over of discipleship in community – the gospel of the Kingdom of God on earth, the proclaimed and implemented mission of the *Logos* made flesh that dwelt amongst us.

6. A Comparison – Farewell Discourses of the Buddha

6.1 Foreword[7]

No doubt my readers may well be familiar with the historical placing and context of the words of Jesus (*ipsissima verba* – exact words, and *ipsissima vox* – exact voice) and the presence of Jesus' teaching. However, some may well be unfamiliar with the words of the Buddha in a similar context. It is commonly accepted that the words of the Buddha (*Buddha vaccana*) when he knew death was at hand are in the *Pali Tipitaka* (the earliest canon orally settled some 80 days after the demise of the Buddha somewhere around 400 BCE), at the first[8] of six Councils of Elder Disciples.

---

[6] We know that Jesus had earmarked Peter for leadership (Matt 16.18-19).

[7] John Vincent, the Leader of the Ashram Community, welcomes my resolved commitment to discipleship to Jesus and simultaneously to the Buddha. In my personal path they are not contradictory. However, I do not advocate this broadly to others.

[8] The last held Council was the sixth, convened at Kaba Aye in Yangon, Myanmar (formerly Rangoon, Burma) in 1954.

6.2 The Mahaparinibbana Sutta

It is also called the "Book of the Great Decease" – *maha* means "great" in both Pali and Sanskrit, while *parinibbana*[9] is more difficult to translate. In the context of this writing I would not hesitate to translate it to mean "liberation in death"; perhaps, it may be akin to the Johannine Jesus' concept of "everlasting life"? The Pali term *sutta* derives from the Sanskrit *sutra*, meaning here a text in aphorism form as opposed to a *shashtra*, meaning a treatise.

Running to some 24,000 words in English translations, it is contained in the collection of Long Discourses of the Buddha, known as the *Digha Nikaya* (long volume) at DN 16 and in the Oxford Pali Text Society (PTS) translation at D ii 72.

The text relates to the last three months of the Buddha's life and it is mostly a conversation-like discourse between the Buddha and Ananda (the beloved younger disciple quite similar to John in relation to Jesus). Given the length of the text we will not address it fully, but only dwell on issues that the Buddha addressed in commonality with Jesus. These are:

1. Discipleship and Community
2. Preparedness for Separation
3. Continuing Community
4. Leadership Provisions
5. Parting Words of Love

6.3 Contextual background

The Buddha and his monastic disciples,[10] both monks and nuns, were mendicants who by intention and rule had no private property apart from their "eight requisites".[11] They lived on alms of food[12] and had no common purse. It must be remembered that the Buddha came from a royal household and as tradition has it, he was also the champion of the realm in all disciplines of the times. Hence, even after renunciation, he commanded respect and support not only from the poor but also from

---

[9] See Pali Text Society – Pali-English Dictionary – http://dsalsrv02.uchicago.edu/cgi-bin/philologic/search3advanced?dbname=pali&query=+parinibb%C4%81na&matchtype=exact&display=utf8

[10] The Buddha had four categories of disciples – *Bhikkhus* (almsmen), *Bhikkhunis* (almswomen), *Upasakas* (laymen) and *Upasikas* (laywomen).

[11] These are the eight basic necessary items. They are: (1) an outer robe, (2) an inner robe, (3) a thick double robe for winter, (4) an alms bowl for gathering food, (5) a razor for shaving, (6) a needle and thread, (7) a belt and (8) a water strainer for removing impurities from drinking water.

[12] This was (and perhaps is) a common practice among various ascetic sects in the Indian subcontinent, well accepted by society.

the wealthy and princely sectors. Yet, he and his disciples, living in nu-merous and "sovereign" microcommunites were units which were com-pletely independent from the conventional socio-political economic establishment, always leading an alternative (contrary to oppositional) way of life with its different morality, laws and rules, and socio-political economic structure. In fact it was an alternative culture – certainly not a counter-culture. For the Buddha and his discipleship communities, the sole and clearly exclusive identity had to be with the dynamic and itin-erant community in discipleship, and so, it was a contradiction in terms to have any loyalty to territory, state, nation, race, clan, or even religion, whatever the circumstances. Similarly, I have yet to find any words at-tributed to the lips of Jesus which indicate otherwise.

6.4 Discipleship and Community

It is obvious that that like Jesus, the Buddha was deeply concerned with the survival of discipleship by having followers of his teachings with con-fidence and without any doubt. Apart from the aforementioned serious, challenging and somewhat difficult undertakings Jesus "demanded" of Peter (entailing other immediate disciples and all those to follow), we know that Jesus' words evidence that if he was still around, the disciples would not stand on their own feet.[13] Also see Jesus' emphasis to observe his teaching at Matt 28.20.

Similarly, the Buddha's concern with survival of discipleship is clearly emphasised in this Sutta:

> Now the Blessed One spoke to the Venerable Ananda saying: "It may be, Ananda, that to some among you the thought will come: 'Ended is the word of the Master; we have a Master no longer.' But it should not, Ananda, be so considered. For that which I have proclaimed and made known as the Dhamma (teaching) and the Vinaya (discipline) that shall be your Master when I am gone". After three times of repetition in similar terms the some 500 disciples remained silent. Then the Buddha said: "It may be, disciples, out of respect for the Master that you ask no questions. Then, disciples, let friend communicate it to friend (who will convey the question to me)." Yet still the disciples were silent. Then the Blessed One addressed the disciples: "It may be, disciples that one of you is in doubt or perplexity as to the Buddha (Enlightenment), the Dhamma (Teaching), or the Sangha (Disci-pleship Community), the path or the practice. Then question, disciples! Do not be given to remorse later on with the thought: The Master was with us face to face, yet face to face we failed to ask him." After three times of similar questioning the disciples were silent.

> Then the Venerable Ananda spoke to the Blessed One, saying: "Marvellous it is, O Lord, most wonderful it is! This faith I have in the community of

[13] See John 14.16, 26; 15.26; 16.7.

disciples that not even one disciple is in doubt or perplexity as to the Buddha (Enlightenment), the Dhamma (Teaching), or the Sangha (Discipleship Community), the path or the practice." However, the Buddha replies: "Out of *faith*, Ananda, you speak thus. But here, Ananda, the enlightened one *knows* for certain that among this community of disciples there is not even one disciple who is in doubt or perplexity…"

6.5 Preparedness for Separation

In both Jesus and the Buddha, there is a clear comprehension of parting, acceptance and giving in to death at the right time and resultant profitability of mission. It is absolutely clear that several attempts were made to kill Jesus from his babyhood up to his crucifixion. Although the Buddha had no such hands-on attempts at being assassinated, there were abortive saboteur attempts made by the princely ruler Ajasatta in collusion with a disciple of the Buddha, Devadatta, who was an elder cousin expressing malice towards the Buddha from childhood.

> "Yet, Ananda, have I not taught from the very beginning that with all that is dear and beloved there must be change, separation, and severance? Of that which is born, come into being, is compounded and subject to decay, how can one say: 'May it not come to dissolution!' There can be no such state of things … my word has been spoken once and for all … Three months hence I will utterly pass away. And that I should withdraw my words for the sake of living on – this is an impossibility."

6.6 Continuing Community

The key here is reinforcement, not recall.

> The growth of the discipleship community is to be expected, not their decline, disciples, so long as you: assemble frequently … ; meet and disperse peacefully and attend to the affairs of the Community in concord; appoint no new rules, and do not abolish the existing ones, but proceed in accordance with the code of training (Vinaya) … respect, honour, esteem, and venerate the elder disciples, those of long standing, long gone forth, the fathers and leaders of the Community, and think it worthwhile to listen to them; so long as they do not come under the power of the craving that leads to fresh becoming; cherish natural habitats for their dwellings; establish themselves in mindfulness … ; so long, disciples, as these seven conditions leading to welfare endure among the disciples and they are known for it … so long as they cultivate the seven factors of enlightenment, that is: mindfulness, investigation into phenomena, energy, bliss, tranquillity, concentration, and equanimity; so long as they attend on each other with lovingkindness in deed, word, and thought, both openly and in private; in respect of what they receive as due offerings, even the contents of their alms bowls, they do not make use of them without sharing them with the community;

in company with their brethren, they train themselves, openly and in private, in the rules of conduct, which are complete and perfect, spotless and pure, liberating, praised by the wise, uninfluenced (by mundane concerns), and favourable to concentration of mind; and in company with their brethren, preserve, openly and in private, the insight that is noble and liberating, and leads one who acts upon it to the utter destruction of suffering.

6.7 Leadership Provisions

"Formerly, Lord ... the disciples would set forth to see you, and to us there was the gain and benefit of receiving and associating with those very revered disciples who came to have audience with you ... But, Lord, after you are gone, we shall no longer have that gain and benefit." Thus spoke the Venerable Ananda.

But the Blessed One answered him, saying: "What more does the community of disciples expect from me, Ananda? I have set forth the Dhamma without making any distinction of esoteric and exoteric doctrine; there is nothing, Ananda ... that I hold to the last with the closed fist of a teacher who keeps some things back. Whosoever may think that it is he who should lead the community of disciples, or that the community depends upon him, it is such a one that would have to give instructions respecting them. But, Ananda, I had no such idea as that it is he who should lead the community of disciples, or that the community depends upon him. So what instructions should he have to give respecting the community of disciples?"

"Now I am frail, Ananda, old, aged, far gone in years. This is my eightieth year, and my life is spent ... Therefore, Ananda, be islands unto yourselves, refuges unto yourselves, seeking no external refuge; with the Dhamma as your island, the Dhamma as your refuge, seeking no other refuge."

6.8 Parting Words of Love

"... But, Ananda, whatever disciple – monk, nun, layman or laywoman, abides by the Dhamma, lives uprightly in the Dhamma, walks in the way of the Dhamma, it is by such a one that the Buddha is respected, venerated, esteemed, worshipped, and honoured in the highest degree."

Then the Venerable Ananda said: "How should we act, Lord, respecting your body?" "Do not hinder yourselves, Ananda, to honour my body. Rather you should strive, Ananda, and be zealous on your own behalf, for your own good. Unflinchingly, ardently, and resolutely you should apply yourselves to your own good."

Then the Blessed One spoke to the Venerable Ananda, saying: "Enough, Ananda! Do not grieve, do not lament! For have I not taught from the very beginning that with all that is dear and beloved there must be change, separation, and severance? Of that which is born, come into being, compounded, and subject to decay, how can one say: 'May it not come to dissolution!'? There can be no such state of things. Now for a long time, Ananda, you have served me with loving-kindness in deed, word, and thought, graciously, pleasantly, with a whole heart and beyond measure. Great good have you gathered, Ananda! Now you should put forth energy, and soon you too will be free from the taints."

Buddha's last words were:

Transient are all compounded things, subject to arising and dying; having come into existence they pass away; good is the peace when they forever cease. Try to accomplish your aim with diligence!

Bibliography

Bouquet, A.C. 1953, *Everyday Life in New Testament Times* (London: B.T. Batsford)

Davies, Helen & Fernando, Nirmal. 2014, *Community*, Pocket Radicals 2 (Sheffield: Ashram Press)

Vincent, John J. 1984, *OK, Let's be Methodists* (London: Epworth Press)

——, ed. 2011 *Christian Communities*. (Sheffield: Ashram Press)

Wesley, John. 1754, *Explanatory Notes Upon the New Testament* (London: Epworth Press, 1976)

Mahaparinibbana Sutta, Long Discourses of the Buddha, *Digha Nikaya*, DN 16 and in the Oxford Pali Text Society (PTS) translation at D ii 72.

10

John: Charter of Cultural Liberation

ALAN SAXBY

The oft-quoted description of the Fourth Gospel by Origen as "The Spiritual Gospel" not only highlights its distinctiveness from the Markan family of texts but also resonates with the experience of generations of Christian readers in more recent literate societies who find it speaking to, affirming and enriching their deepest inner selves. In truth, it is *the* Mystical Gospel speaking at depth to those who open themselves to its words.

But, as with all literature, a clearly perceived focus on one thesis can result in other dimensions and agendas being marginalised or pushed beyond even peripheral awareness – a gestalt effect. This is the danger presented by this word of Origen, for the Gospel according to John is anything but a single issue – it is complex and richly multi-layered. It further displays signs of still being a "work-in-progress", not only in the evidence of textual instability (the woman taken in adultery, 7.53–8.11) and narrative development (the "epilogue" of ch. 21) but also the occurrence of "loose" editing such as remnants of a futurist eschatology (e.g. 5.25-29; 6.35-59) embedded in a writing which consistently foregrounds realised eschatology as a major theme (e.g. 3.17-21; 5.24; 11.23-27).

We should not be over-critical as we sit at our laptops. Producing a fully coherent and consistent document with a technology base of scrolls and handwriting, working with scripts that know neither punctuation nor word division is no easy task. Further, the Gospel writers were also part of a culture where orality still ruled, and orality does not encourage precision and accuracy, for every rendition (even written) is a fresh performance.

These features are all part of John's Gospel being "work-in-process": we are in touch with a faith seeking to readdress itself in a world that has rapidly become very different from that in which the Jesus traditions were birthed. A familiar challenge.

The Central Issue

The very fact that John is a "Gospel" inevitably earths it in the story of Jesus as its foundational script. With a strong consensus that John writes at a later date than the Synoptics, the very evident gulf between his contact with that earlier tradition and the very distinctive content that fills most of his narrative has led to much debate as to whether John knew any of the other canonical trio. And if he did, was he seeking to correct or to supplement them? Such investigations into the interrelationships of the Gospels are necessary, but only as background to the central issue of the Fourth Gospel itself. Even if John occasionally betrays awareness of arguably better traditions than those underlying the Synoptics, such as the relation of the Last Supper to the date of the Passover, the key issue remains: What do we make of this apparently very different Jesus? Allowing a general presumption that the Synoptic accounts are the closest thing we have to what this Galilean peasant did and said, the question confronting us is: What does John do with this "Jesus of History"?

It is a question that is compounded by the very ambiguity embedded in his presentation:

- On the one hand from the programmatic prologue, rising to its climax in the affirmation that "the Word became flesh" (1.1-18) through to the dying scene of the crucifixion with its eye-witness who "knows that he tells the truth" (19.35) John emphasises the very earthy reality of the life of Jesus who is flesh and blood.

- Yet on the other hand, even though he weeps at the grave of a friend (11.35) and is disturbed by the foreknowledge of his imminent betrayal by Judas (13.21) there is nothing in the fourth Gospel approaching the sheer *angst* of Gethsemane. Jesus typically moves serenely through John's narration as the Son of God, and John's skill as a dramatist is never more clearly evident than in the trial scene before Pilate where Jesus, as the one being judged, bestrides the scene as The Judge. More than this, in marked distinction from the Synoptic Gospels, John, having affirmed the sheer physicality of Jesus, then seems to play "fast and loose" with the details (e.g. dislocating the Temple-Cleansing story from its integral part in the Passion Narrative). But that is to move ahead of ourselves.

John and the "Old, Old Story"

That there are interconnections between the Synoptics and John, from obvious Sabbath healing (5.1-18) to the more intriguing Lazarus / "if one should rise" linkage (11.1-53/Luke 16.19-31), can hardly be doubted. Some awareness of Lukan tradition is evident, but Mark's Gospel has been the most popular candidate as a literary resource for John's writing: for example in the story of the Anointing at Bethany (Mark 14.3-9; Matt 26.6-13; John 12.1-8) – definitely the same event – where John's repetition of the very rare word πιστικῆς ("pure/genuine") from Mark (not used by Matthew) argues strongly for a knowledge of Mark's work. However, in the story as a whole the amount of verbal identity with Mark (the key test of literary dependency) is small and largely restricted to those features of the story which are pretty well demanded by the story itself.

What is more impressive is that John frames his account of the ministry of Jesus around incidents, labelled as "Signs", all of which have their roots in the earlier gospel traditions but are characteristically "born anew" in the hands of John.

Some of these "Signs" are very familiar:

- Cleansing the Temple (2.13-22), although the setting is transposed from that of the Passion story;
- Feeding of the 5,000 (6.1-59);
- Anointing at Bethany (12.1-7);
- Triumphal Entry into Jerusalem (12.12-19).

Others clearly echo synoptic stories, though lacking precise identification:

- Jesus heals an official's son at a distance (4.46-53) – which resonates with the story of healing the Centurion's servant (Matt. 8.5-13; Luke 7.1-10).
- Healing a cripple at the pool of Bethzatha on the Sabbath (5.2-18) – resonance with the healing of the paralytic (Mark 2.1-12; Matt 9.1-8; Luke 5.17-26); healing the man with the crippled hand (Mark 3.1-6; Matt. 12.9-14; Luke 6.6-11);
- Healing a blind man (9.1-41) – resonance with healing the blind man at Bethsaida (Mark 8.22-26) and Sabbath-healing stories such as the man with the crippled hand (above); also, healing two blind men (Matt. 9.27-31) and Bartimaeus (Mark 10.46-52; Matt. 20.29-34; Luke 18.35-43).

Whilst a few are created out of recognizable synoptic material:

- Turning water into wine (2.1-11) – dramatising the saying about new wine (Mark 2.22; Matt. 9.17; Luke 5.37-39).
- Raising of Lazarus (11.1-53) – a complex setting, given that it is the resurrection of Jesus himself that is the sign of the victory of life over death (11.25). John proleptically brings this into the

"present" of the ministry of Jesus, drawing on the story of Lazarus (Luke 16.19-31) with its ending of "neither will they be
convinced even if someone rises from the dead" along with ech-
oes of the Stone and the Tomb of the first Easter morning narrative (Mark 15.46–16.4; Matt. 27.59-61; Luke 24.2; cf. John
11.38-39).

I consider the evidence for John being familiar with the *scripts* of Mark
and Luke (the two strongest candidates) is fragile: however, it is clear
that he was fully cognizant with those clusters of early Christian tradition
about Jesus that also surface within the Synoptic record. His read-
ers/hearers would also be familiar with them. But who was his audience?

The World of the Fourth Evangelist

With the exception of Luke (Luke 1.1-4) none of the Gospels tell us
who their audience is. We have to work it out from evidence within
the writings themselves – and therein lies the rub: over the years scholars
have posited a range of "audiences", including the world of Hellenism
(particularly that represented by Philo), some form of sectarian Judaism,
or an emergent Gnosticism (or should that be "gnosticism"?). Connec-
tions with Mesopotamian religious terminology in the Mandaean literature have been explored, and the Dead Sea Scrolls occasioned a re-think.

Whatever – the important point is that John was living in a very different world and clearly writing *for a very different audience* than that of
either Galilee in the time of Jesus, or the initial recipients of Mark, Matthew and Luke's writings.

Although, as we have seen, his story is rooted in the much earlier
Christian tradition, his audience is living in a much broader world of
ideas and understanding than that of pre-70 Galilee or Jerusalem. The
original formatting of the Christian message (including the message of
Jesus) within the thought-world of late second-temple Judaism with its
belief in the imminence of the End ushering in the Kingdom of God
could only be held onto with difficulty. The exhortations woven into
the Synoptics' fabric to persevere and stay alert "for no man knows the
time" are a fossil remnant of this time of tension and diminishing hope.

But the Markan Jesus *had* assured his hearers that "there are some
standing here who will not taste death until they see that the kingdom
of God has come with power" (Mark 9.1). The first part of that prophecy proved false – what were (or are) the odds of the second half still
occurring (then or now)?

Luke eventually took the pragmatic approach and put the whole issue on the "back-burner" (Acts 1.7-8)

John grasped the nettle.

"He is ahead of you"

The message of the young man at the empty tomb to the women early on that first Easter morning (Mark 16.7) could almost describe John's response. Just as both his enemies and his friends thought that Jesus was contained within the confines of the tomb, so the early Church proclaimed Jesus through the medium and largely within the confines of the thought world and cultural orientation of late second-temple Judaism. Even beyond its Palestinian homeland it was within that same "extended" world – Jewish communities gathered around their synagogue, with their Gentile adherents – that the early Christian missioners found their most ready response, as the book of Acts clearly demonstrates.

It was the world of their primary socialisation, as it had been of Jesus himself. It provided the language and conceptual framework within which his followers, quite naturally, came to terms with the impact of Jesus' life and interpreted his message and teaching. It continued to provide that understanding through the succeeding decades, but with increasing tension as the years passed:

- the generation of "witnesses" succumbed to their mortality whilst world history lumbered on in its time-honoured fashion;
- and, with the Church of Jerusalem decimated in the war of 66–70 CE, the centre of gravity of the Christian movement moved into (and beyond?) the Diaspora with Gentile membership an increasingly significant factor.

Throughout the Apostolic and Sub-Apostolic period the message of Jesus continued to be proclaimed within that same framework, honed in Roman-occupied Israel, even as that world view was being abandoned by the founding rabbis of early Formative Judaism. There was talk of holding true to "the faith once delivered" (Jude 3), and the writer of 2 Peter well into the second century, a hundred years after Paul, is still affirming the imminent "day of the Lord" as an incentive for Christian living (2 Peter 3.8-18).

John broke out of this conceptual frame within which Jesus had been proclaimed and interpreted. With boldness he re-told the gospel story (still very recognizable as the "gospel story") for a world that was both culturally and intellectually broader and very different from the Galilee of Jesus' day.

John no longer looks ahead in anticipation (or dread) of a final Judgment Day and the "Second Coming" of Christ – Christ *has* come in all his fullness, there is no more. The End, the time of fulfilment, is *now* – and always in our "now". In the light of his presence we experience *now* both condemnation and the present gift of eternal life (3.16-21):

- judgment and salvation do not await us on the Last Day (11.23-26) but are an existential reality now in the presence of the Christ who, as the "light coming into the world" (1.9), simultaneously attracts to that light whilst repelling darkness (3.17-21) – in that Presence we know our own sinfulness and failure but also receive   the vision of our own potential (dramatised in the Sign of the Man Born Blind [9.1-41]).
- John replaces the "temporal" distinction between "this present age" and the "age to come" in the Judaic framework of the Synoptics by the almost Platonic "spatial" distinction between the "world below" and the "world above";
- the focal phrase of Jesus' preaching in the Synoptics – "Kingdom of God" (Mark 1.14 etc.) – is almost completely replaced with "eternal life";
- the "Son of Man" is no longer an apocalyptic figure coming on the clouds to usher in the Final Day but a description of the One who has come "from above" and will return there as he is "lifted up" on the cross (12.32-33).

In opening ourselves to his words, his story, his presence we find ourselves acutely aware of our own deficiencies and failings while feeling called and empowered by visions of a new self and a new world.

We have already noted that fragments of the earlier way of thinking can still be found in uneasy tension with the new, but this may not be careless editing: it also points to the great difficulty we all have in casting off a deeply ingrained mental paradigm (which, in this case, is still present with us and haunts us).

Change the Paradigm

John telegraphs his radical re-interpretation and re-presentation of the Christian message in the opening prologue (1.1-14). Drawing on imagery from both Judaic and Hellenistic worlds he recapitulates the salvation-history of God's people (thereby re-affirming the roots of the Christian movement) coming to fulfilment when "the *Logos* became flesh ... and we beheld his glory". In the original framing of the Christian message (e.g. Phil. 2.6-11) there had been a strong contrast between the

lowliness of the human Jesus and the glory that is his following his res-
urrection/ascension/return to the Father. It is only for a few brief moments on the Mount of Transfiguration in the Synoptic record that Jesus'
glory was disclosed during his earthly ministry (Mark 9.2-8).

John is asserting that if only we take the time and the trouble to shift
our position and view the "old, old story" from within a different framework, a changed paradigm, we shall begin to see that it was not just for
a few fleeting moments that "his glory" was revealed but it is present in
everything he was and did. That narrative opening to his "first sign"
(2.1) is much more than a diary reference – "On the third day ..." – a
phrase redolent with Easter associations from the earliest time (1 Cor.
15.4 etc.). Everything Jesus did in the Christian story is a "Sign" of the
meaning and significance of his whole life, peaking in his dying/rising.

There is a real sense in which Origen was right – John probes beneath
and beyond the surface of the received narrative tradition into its potential depths. John's focus is on the "now" of our existence as the only
moment of reality, and invests it with absolute significance in the flood-
light of a Christ who both attracts and disturbs, in whose light we pro-
nounce judgement on ourselves, yet who calls and confers on us new
possibilities of living.

A Charter of Liberation

"Raised ... not here ... ahead of you". Not only could death not hold
him (Acts 2.24) – never mind Joseph of Arimathea's tomb – but neither
can our words, cultural traditions, intellectual understandings or inter-
pretive frameworks. Although deeply rooted in the foundation traditions
of the Christian movement, John boldly and radically reinterpreted and
re presented that tradition into a different framework and symbolic uni-
verse, with fragments of the discarded frame being carried along in the
flow. Whilst remaining in touch with the traditions that gave birth to
the movement, he avoided the dead-end of futilely trying to hang on to
familiar words and patterns of thinking that were increasingly "out of
sync" with a radically changed world. Jesus, as ever, had gone on ahead
where John discovered him afresh. In his writing John liberated the
Christian tradition from the developing straitjacket of its historical culture and transposed it into that of the world in which he and his audience
lived.

Little wonder that it took the Church significantly longer to accept
John's work alongside that of Matthew, Mark and Luke. But it is important that, aside from this early hesitancy, John has stood four-square
within the Christian canon of scripture. John's Gospel is our charter of
Christian intellectual freedom – and it stands within the Bible itself as
one of our "fab four" as an exemplar of how each generation has to be

prepared to continually rethink and restructure its story within ever-changing historical scenarios and cultures.

Whenever a faith is feeling the strain of maintaining itself within a dynamically developing culture and vigorous intellectual exploration there is always the temptation to cling with increasing tenacity to the old and familiar. That was true in the dying years of the first century: it is true today, as witnessed by the rising tide of assertive Christian and Islamic fundamentalism. That was not John's way. He let the tradition speak to him, living within a very different world from that of its origin, and with thought and imagination he shared the Christ he glimpsed. We must do the same in our postmodern, high-tech, multi-cultural, multi-faith, globalised world.

For us, too, the story of Jesus remains the launch pad for this herme-neutical exploration. It is a high-risk strategy. There is every possibility that we will get it significantly wrong. There is that ever present danger that we shall discover a Christ made in our own image.

John does provide some guidance. His Christ is the one in whose very presence in our "now" we find ourselves both judged and set free. A Christ we feel comfortable with is one to mistrust. The Christ that is true to our tradition is the one who challenges, disturbs and unsettles. Yet, curiously, at the same time empowers us with visions of hope and of what can be.

He is always there – ahead of us.

A Practice Interpretation Bibliography

Davies, Helen, and Fernando, Nirmal, 2014. *Community. Pocket Radicals 2*. Sheffield: Ashram Press

Davies, John D. 2013. "Inclusion in the Acts of the Apostles", *Expository Times*, 124.4, 167-176

Francis, Leslie J., 1997. "Personality Type and Scripture: Exploring Mark's Gospel". London: Mowbray

Holgate, David and Starr, Rachel, 2006. *SCM Study Guide to Biblical Hermeneutics*. London: SCM Press

Hooker, Morna D., & Vincent, John J., 2010. *The Drama of Mark*. London: Epworth Press

Horrell, David G., 2012. *The Bible and the Environment*. London: Equinox/Acumen

Houston, Fleur, 2015. *Love the Stranger as Yourself. The Bible. Refugees and Asylum*. London: Routledge

Houston, Walter, 2010. *Justice: The Biblical Challenge*. London: Equinox/Acumen

Lawrence, Louise J. 2009. " 'The Stilling of the Sea' and the Imagination of Place in a Cornish Fishing Village", *Expository Times* 120. 4, 172-177

—— , 2004, " 'On a Cliff's Edge': Actualising Lk. 8.22-39" *Expository Times* 119.3, 111-115.

—— , 2009. *The Word in Place*, London: SPCK

Miller, Susan, 2004. *Women in Mark's Gospel*. London/New York: T&T Clark International

Riches, John, 2005. "John J. Vincent's 'Outworkings'". *Expository Times* 116.5, 153-154

——, 2010. *Contextual Bible Study*. London: SPCK

Rogerson, J.W., ed., 2014. *Leviticus in Practice*, Blandford Forum: Deo Publishing

—— and Vincent, John, 2009. *The City in Biblical Perspective*. London: Equinox/Acumen

—— and Clout, Imogen, 2014. *More Places at the Table. Legal and Biblical Perspectives on Modern Family Life*. Sheffield: Feed a Read.

—— and Vincent, John, eds., 2016. *The Servant of God*. Blandford Forum: Deo Publishing (forthcoming).

Rowland, Christopher and Vincent, John, eds., 2013. *For Church and Nation: British Liberation Theology 5*. Sheffield: Urban Theology Unity

—— and Roberts, Jonathan, 2008. *Bible for Sinners; Interpretation in the Present Time*. London: SPCK

Vincent, John, 2015. *Radical Jesus: The Way of Jesus, Then and Now.* 3rd ed. Sheffield: Ashram Press

——, 2004. "Theological Practice", *Theology*, Sept–Oct, 343–350.

——, 2005. *Outworkings: Gospel Practice and Interpretation.* Sheffield: Urban Theology Unit

——, ed., 2006. *Mark: Gospel of Action. Personal and Community Responses.* London: SPCK

——, 2007. *Discipleship. Pocket Radicals 1.* Sheffield: Ashram Press

——, ed., 2011. *Stilling the Storm: Contemporary Responses to Mark 4.35–5.1.* Blandford Forum: Deo Publishing

——, ed., 2012, *Acts in Practice.* Blandford Forum: Deo Publishing

——, ed., 2016. *Discipleship.* Blandford Forum: Deo Publishing

——, "Outworkings" *Expository Times*

——, 2001: "A Gospel Practice Criticism," 113.1, 16–18

——, 2002: "Gospel Practice Today", 113.11, 367–371

——, 2005: "The Practice of Disciples" (Mark 2), 119.12, 587–588

——, 2006: "Disciple Practice Today" (Mark 2), 118.7, 326–330

——, 2008: "Twelve as Christian Community" (Mark 3), 119.12, 582–588

——, 2011: "Urban Mission in Mark 4", 122.11, 541–538

——, 2013: "Multi-Faith Mission in Mark 5", 125.3, 117–122

——, 2013, *Christ in the City: the Dynamics of Christ in Urban Theological Practice.* Sheffield: Urban Theology Unit

——, ed. 2015. *Radical Christianity: Roots and Fruits.* Sheffield. St Mark's Centre for Radical Christianity Press

Wallis, Ian, 2000. *Holy Saturday Faith: Rediscovering the Legacy of Jesus.* London: SPCK

West, Gerald, 2007. *Reading Otherwise: Socially engaged Biblical Scholars Reading with their Local Communities.* Atlanta: Society of Biblical Literature

—— & Zengele Bungi, 2011. "Time for Jesus to Wake Up", in Vincent, ed., pp. 97–106.

For earlier work, see the Bibliography in Vincent, ed., 2006, 202.

Index of Subjects and Names

Abiding 38, 43, 58, 59
Academy 12, 13
Acts of Jesus 10, 11, 65-66
Alongside, Horizontal 16, 17, 39,
    68-70
Apprenticeship 61
Ashton, J. 14, 16

Barrett, C.K. 50, 66, 68
Barth, K. 14
British New Testament Confer-
    ence 12-13
Brown, R.E. 50, 51
Buddin, Farewell Discourse 77-82
Bultmann, R. 52

Cadbury, H.J. 68
Capper, B.J. 52, 53
Church Times 14
Community, Johannine 15, 16,
    54, 66, 67-68, 70, 83, 86-88
Common, Things in 26, 50, 53,
    73, 76
Community of Disciples 11, 12,
    33, 53, 54, 67, 69, 70, 73-77
Crucifixion 30-33, 55, 84

Davies, P.R. 53
Disciples and Jesus 35, 38-39, 45,
    55-60, 65-70, 73-76
Discipleship 14, 34, 63, 64, 70-71,
    73-74
Divinisation 18, 69, 70
Dodd, C.H. 64, 69

Embodiment 11, 15, 16, 55, 56,
    68-70
Endogenous Analysis 13
Eschatology 83, 86-88
Essenes 40, 41, 51-53
Expository Times 13

Faith Training 30, 61, 63, 71-72
Father, Jesus, Spirit 17, 68-71

Glory 16, 69, 89
Gods, Humans as 67, 69, 70, 71
Gospel of Peter 57

Handing on 16, 59-60, 65-66
Hermeneutics 12, 21, 90
Holgate D. 46, 47
Hospitality 54, 61, 63, 73
Howard-Brook, W. 15, 66, 67

Imitation of God 11, 16, 67
Imitation of Jesus 11, 17, 56, 65,
    70-71
Inner-City Retreat 72
Intentional Community 63, 73, 77

Jesus in John 32, 34-35, 49-50,
    65-66, 73-74, 84-89
Jesus' work continued in Disciples
    55-56, 61, 65-66, 89
John, Purpose of 15, 16, 35, 51,
    83, 84
Josephus 51, 58-59
Jeremias, J. 50

Kingdom of God on Earth 77, 87-89

Last Supper 52, 56-57, 60, 84
Leadership 26, 76
Ling, T. 53
Love 33, 58, 63, 69, 76-77

Management 44-45
Minear, P.S. 70

Nicodemus 34

Opposition, Persecution 59-60
Origen 83, 89
Outworkings 13, 68-70

Paraclete 15, 17, 59, 68
Peter 32, 74-77
Pickstock, C. 14
Poor, Ministry to 63, 73
Practice 11-12, 17, 60-61, 65-66, 66-68
Practice Interpretation 12-14, 16-17, 27, 55
Presence of Jesus 18, 55, 60-61
Psychological Type 21-28, 42

Radical Christianity 13
Rensberger, D. 67
Research Excellence Framework 14
Resurrection 59, 61, 74, 85-86, 89
Revelation 69, 70-71
Righteousness 11, 29-30, 53
Robinson, J.A.T. 76
Rogerson, J.W. 7, 12

Schnackenburg, R. 49
Schneider, S.M. 16
Servant of God 7, 26
Servants, Disciples as 24-27, 67
Stevick, D. 70
Synoptics and John 34-35, 56-58, 60, 65, 75, 83-87

Temple 30, 50, 53, 54
Temple Cleansing 30, 31, 51, 84

Theresa of Avila 72

Use and Influence 11, 12
Use of John's Gospel 12-13

Way, Truth and Life 63, 69
Watson, F. 16
Wesley, J. 79
Wisdom 45, 61, 63
World 34-36, 39-40, 43-46, 65, 86-87
Works of Jesus 66-68,
Worship 61-62

Printed in the United States
by Baker & Taylor Publisher Services

Printed in the United States
by Baker & Taylor Publisher Services